THROUGH MY EYES...

THROUGH MY EYES...

by

ANDRÉ NIRENBERGER

Through My Eyes...

Author's photograph on the back cover by Linda Tawney

Library of Congress Control Number: 2008909521

ISBN: 978-0-615-25729-7

Through My Eyes... is dedicated to my parents, Leon and Leokadia Nirenberger.

My Loving Mom and Dad,

Because of you, I am.

You gave me life and protected me during World War II.

Dad, when the war broke out not long after I was born, you were in France overseeing that branch of our textile business. While Mom was keeping me safe in Poland, you were doing what you could from afar to reunite us as a family. You hardly knew me, and sadly, I did not remember you. We did not meet again until I was nine years old and I called you "Sir" even though you were my dad. At that time, I did not understand that you were hurt by being called "Sir." I know now that we missed what perhaps could have been our best times.

Mom, you are my best friend, even though you are no longer among us. I am alive today because you shielded me from our enemies. It is only now that I understand the enormity of your sacrifice during the horrible war. For me, you are not gone. You have just left for a faraway place that, for now, I cannot reach.

Both of you gave me the best you could. You provided me with a good education. You introduced me to many cultures in different countries. Most of all, you both put up with my begging letters when I was attending boarding schools. I was always writing, "Give me, give me, give me..." And you always did.

When I was a boy, I had dreams. One of them was to build a castle for Mom. That never happened. I always wanted a brother or sister, but that was not to be. I regret that when I was younger I was not aware of how much you gave of yourselves to protect me until I grew up and left home.

I love you both for many reasons. Alas, I cannot hug you now, but you are still part of my life.

Rest in peace, my beautiful ones.

May God bless you.

Que Dieu vous guarde.

Pobłogosław Boze drogi.

Que Dios los bendiga.

Your son,
André

TABLE OF CONTENTS

Acknowledgments   ix

Part One: Bombs, Butter, and Boarding School   1

Chapter 1   How Did The *Krasnoludki* Know?   3

Chapter 2   My Mother, Leokadia Mackiewicz   7

Chapter 3   My Father, Leon Nirenberger   13

Chapter 4   On The Run   17

Chapter 5   Safe In Sweden   23

Chapter 6   Almost There   27

Chapter 7   Reunited in France   29

Chapter 8   The Wrong Uniform!   35

Chapter 9   École des Roches   39

Chapter 10   Christmas in Vigneux   45

Chapter 11   Returning to Switzerland   51

Chapter 12   Suisse Summers   57

Chapter 13   École St. Augustin   67

Chapter 14   Vigneux Friendships   77

Chapter 15   Three Trips into the Unknown   85

Part Two: Talents, Travails, and Triumphs   95

Chapter 16   Through My Eyes...   97

Chapter 17   What Next?   115

Chapter 18   Coming to America   125

Chapter 19   My Country Now   137

Chapter 20   Creating the Salons   145

Chapter 21   AlexAndré Coiffure   153

Chapter 22   Mr. André Salon   159

Part Three: Family, Fortitude, and Fulfillment   **165**

Chapter 23   A Family, At Last   167

Chapter 24   The Children's Challenges   173

Chapter 25   On The Radar   185

Chapter 26   Auschwitz   191

Chapter 27   Reflections   195

ACKNOWLEDGMENTS

*T*hrough My Eyes... would not have been possible without the involvement of my wife Carolina. Aware of my ambition to write this book for the past twenty years, she opened all the necessary doors for me. Through her support and encouragement, Carolina made sure that I did not quit in the middle, which I have the habit of doing. Thank you, My Darling.

Barbara L. Warren, my instructor in *Writing Your Life's Stories,* soon became my editor and consultant for this book. Barbara, a writer as well as a workshop leader, also facilitates Socrates Café. Now that Barbara has finished editing my book, she can devote time to her own books, *Rainbows of Memories: Healing During Loss* and *MOMM: Memory of the Month Method.*

Barbara showed me the key to writing. It was so simple that I wondered why I had never thought of it before. She said, "Write the way you talk." I wanted to see if that would work — and it did! Barbara also encouraged me to continue, even when I was faced with solving difficult writing situations. *Merci beaucoup, Mon Amie, pour m'avoir aidè dans ce nouveau chemin.*

Lorraine Louden and Vernita Joy Johnson, the early readers of *Through My Eyes...,* were indispensable in coaxing me to finish writing this book. They were objective enough to see the real story and to tell me what was important and what was not. Lorraine read thoughtfully, asked questions, offered suggestions, and discovered many typos and missing words. Joy's gift of sound led to the chapter titles and to a new awareness of the power of words. I appreciate Joy's comments on the back cover. I owe both Lorraine and Joy a great deal. Thank you, My Friends, for your insights.

Joyce B. Rodrigues researched World War II, including the Polish Underground and Post Traumatic Stress Disorder. From the other side of the country, she taught us to use the computer programs essential for this book. Thank you, My Invisible Friend. Maybe we will meet some day.

Joanna Schwarz, a landscape photographer and musician, saw the cover picture and said, "Look at those eyes." Joanna quickly brainstormed possibilities and came up with the title *Through My Eyes...* Thank you, My Talented Friend, for the perfect title for my book.

For the *pièce de résistance*, I must mention my youngest daughter, Dora M. Mata. I asked her to write what she thought about her dad. At the time, I did not realize that I was putting her in a difficult situation. But, as always, Dora took the task to heart and did a wonderful job. I know that what she wrote is exactly what she thinks. Dora's comments appear in Chapter 24, *On The Radar*. Dora is a straight-forward, no-nonsense person and I love her for that. Thank you, Sweetheart.

And finally, a special Thank You to everyone in Barbara's *Writing Your Life's Stories* workshops --- for listening to my early drafts, for offering suggestions and encouragement, and for believing I could actually write *Through My Eyes...*

Part One

BOMBS BUTTER BOARDING SCHOOL

Chapter 1

I was a young child during World War II, so my recollections are a compilation of vivid remembrances, stories told by my mother, and letters that I found after my father's death. Some memories are like snapshots of events and have no real beginnings or endings. Others seem to unfold in slow motion.

When World War II started, my mother and I were at home in Warsaw, Poland, while my father was overseeing the French branch of our textile business. We didn't realize it then, but we would not be reunited as a family for nearly nine years. During the war, my mother and I often had to join long columns of other displaced people, running from the Germans or the Russians, depending upon which army was winning at the time.

When I was six years old, we lived somewhere in Poland during one respite from all the running. I remember that we stayed in a narrow, white, two-story farm house with a big backyard and a goat. The goat was tied to the side of the house and he always tried to butt me when I passed by. I had a wooden scooter, the kind that needs one foot on the scooter while the other foot pushes. I rode back and forth for days trying to make friends with the goat. Alas, my efforts were to no avail.

A pathway bordered by shrubs about two to three feet high crossed the yard. One day, I scooted along the pathway and stopped at the last shrub. I don't know why I stopped at the last bush. Normally, I just continued my ride and ended up by the front of the house. But that day I had an experience that changed my life. I call this memory *krasnoludki* and, while I know that many people may find it hard to believe, this is what happened that day.

When I stopped at the last shrub, I discovered three *krasnoludki*. I could not tell how they were dressed. However, I understood everything they said. They did not seem to move their lips and I do not remember hearing any sound. Keep in mind that I was six years old and the war was going on. I did not fully understand the implications of the war or its consequences, although I had already seen death.

However, I understood the *krasnoludki's* message. They indicated that I should not be worried: nothing would happen to me and I would be safe.

Telling this story now gives credence to the reality that throughout the war, bombs exploded so close to me that twice my right arm was broken. One bomb fell while my mother and I were running down some flights of stairs to a bomb shelter. The explosion lifted me into the air and slammed me up against a solid wall. When my mother picked me up, she realized that my right arm was broken. After the bombing, a doctor put my arm in a cast. Later, both the cast and my arm were broken during another bombing raid. And yet I survived, just as the *krasnoludki* had promised.

This next part is my mother's story, the way she told it to me. She and I, along with 35 other family members and friends, huddled together in a basement shelter while the Germans bombed Warsaw. A bomb dropped into the chimney and slid all the way to the basement before exploding and killing everyone except my mother and me. Again, the *krasnoludki's* message proved to be true.

Later, my mother and I found ourselves on a train headed to Auschwitz. The train was so crowded that if anyone passed out or died, there was no place for that person to fall. Since I was a young boy, I was not very tall so I had difficulty breathing. A man, who was standing in the corner near a very small window, lifted me to his shoulders so I could breathe. Amazingly, ours was the only train that never reached the concentration camp. The Polish Underground stopped the train and freed us all. How did the *krasnoludki* know I would be saved?

When I grew up to be a teenager in France, I continued to be aware of a presence behind me. I felt that someone or something was always protecting me from danger. This presence remained with me from the time I was six and discovered the *krasnoludki* under the shrub until I was a man in my middle twenties.

Yes, those *krasnoludki* were three leprechauns. This story may be hard to believe. However, I am alive to tell you about what happened then. Many other victims of the war are no longer among us, but I hope they will never be forgotten.

Chapter 2

My mother, Leokadia Mackiewicz, was born on September 10, 1909, in Warsaw, Poland, to a comfortable family. My mother told me many stories. Some I have forgotten. However, a few I remember vividly.

My mother and Eleonora Gurkiewicz had been best friends since the third grade. My mother told me that one day she wanted to dress as a lady in a long, elaborate dress. When her parents were not at home, she and Eleonora decided to take the window drapes down and cut them in the shape of a dress.

Another time she said that she was competing with a friend to see who could spit the furthest from the second story of her house. My mom, not ever wanting to lose, extended herself so much from the window that she fell head-first to the ground below. Her mother found her on the ground and took her to the hospital. My mother said that the top of her head was very soft, and that the only thing she could tell her mother is that she did not do it on purpose.

Later, my mother and Eleonora attended an up-scale boarding school and then university. At that time, going to boarding school and university was only for well-to-do families. Most of the young women of school age were taught how to be good wives rather than getting an education for their future. Eleonora became a very successful dress designer. She also did business with my father, who at that time had not yet met my mother.

Mother was a very active person before she was married. She skied, competed in tobogganing, and enjoyed classical dancing. It is actually during a skiing outing that she met my father. I do not know the date she met my father, since she did not tell me. But she did tell me about the chicken.

Chicken is very important in my life. If it were not for chicken, I might not have been born. My mother and her friend Eleonora belonged to a ski club. One day the group was in the Zakopane Mountains of Poland. My mother and her friend were talking about men, and what kind of men they would like to marry. At that moment, a male club member was passing by. My mother turned to her friend, and said, "I would not mind this one."

That evening, all the club members were having dinner together. The table at which my mother was sitting was a table for 14 people. Everybody was talking about skiing and future good times. When the food was served, chicken was the main course. My mother looked at her plate and found that she had been served a chicken leg, which she did not like. You have to understand that my mother was a very straight-forward person. She was not bashful and she was not afraid to ask for what she wanted.

After pausing for few seconds, she stood up, put her two hands on the table, and looked around to see who had what piece of chicken. She noticed that the man she had seen earlier had a chicken breast on his plate. Without any hesitation, she pointed toward the man's dish, looked him in the eyes, and said in a loud voice, "If you will give me your breast, I will give you my legs." From there, their courtship started.

Later, when my mother and I were in Sweden, she made a lot of friends because of her personality. She also continued to dance and had some parts in community theater plays. She was a good-looking young lady and had several marriage proposals. However, she stayed true to my father.

I must say that during her lifetime she was that same woman who was not bashful. She always went straight to the point. There was never any misunderstanding on my part about what I had to do. I remember one time she told me to always tell the truth and she warned me that if I did anything that would deserve a jail sentence, she would be the first one to put me there.

My mother was a lovely woman, strong, yet very caring and loving. When I was a teenager, she was my best friend. I have the warmest memories of her.

These stories represent my mom's character during her short life. She always liked to do different things. She was a free spirit and she believed that women were as good as anyone, which was *avant-garde* thinking for the times. She was as comfortable being an important well-to-do lady as she was being a woman who had to scrape for survival for her son and herself during the war.

When the Russian Army came to Poland, the Polish population did not trust them at all. In many instances, there were murders, abuse, theft and many other improprieties. Even after the destruction the Germans left behind in Poland, the Russian soldiers still found things that they had never had or had never seen before. There were a lot of women in the Russian Army. Most of these women came from farms and they had not experienced anything outside of their world. That said, a lot of these women went into houses and saw nice things they did not know how to use. So when they found girdles and did not know how to wear them, they put the girdles over their uniforms. The men looked for money, food, or anything else they could barter with.

At one time, my mother and I were living in a house that was surrounded by two others, one on the left and the other on the right. The floor in our house was made of parquet, but it was very old and grey looking. There were only two rooms. The main room included the entrance door. In the middle of the floor, there was a hinged door covered by a small carpet. When opened, the door gave way to a small basement made of hard, black dirt. A small wooden ladder descended into the basement. My mother had a large quantity of potatoes in that basement. I do not know how she got them, but they were the only food that we had to eat.

Someone saw several Russian soldiers coming towards the houses. My mother told me to get out of the house and to go hide with another person in another house. I remember the person was a man. When I arrived at his house, he did not want to take the chance of hiding me, so I went behind the house and stayed very still.

Later on my mother told me that a Russian soldier had come to our house and wanted food. She told him that she did not have any. However, he did not believe her and took her to the other room where we had a bed. He threw her on the bed and took his revolver out and put it to my mother's head. She told me that he held her for over two hours with the revolver to her head, but he never found the potatoes. It didn't dawn on me then, but now that I've had time to think about it, I wonder what else he did. Obviously, my mother never told me if anything else happened.

I am convinced that my mother's belief that nothing was impossible helped us during the war. It seems that both sides of my family were involved in the Underground while Poland was occupied by the Germans.

My cousin Wiesia's father was working as a functionary in the municipal Warsaw consul, while also being a member of an Underground military organization. Wiesia was in the Polish Underground. My paternal uncle Joseph Nirenberger, now Nowicki, was in the Jewish Underground. At that time, the head of the Jewish Underground was Ariel Sharon, who later became Israel's prime minister.

When I was in France few years ago, my cousin Tad Nowicki and I looked at his wedding pictures. I was already living in the United States when he was married in 1962, so I did not participate in his wedding. We came upon a photo that showed my father standing by himself in the first church pew. I questioned Tad about where my mother was. At first he did not want to say anything. However, he eventually confessed that my mother had not been invited. I was astonished. I knew that my mother and his were not on the best of terms, but I never knew why. Only then did I learn that my paternal grandmother and aunt had been killed by the Gestapo. They were thrown from the second floor of their domicile to the street below. Tad's mom blamed my mother because she was convinced that my mother did not use her contacts to save them.

That statement opened another chapter in my search for information about certain happenings during the war that I did not understand. I have a picture of my mother and me on a beach. The question that I often asked myself was, "Where during the war could we have been relaxing on a beach?" My cousin Tad, who is older than I, came up with some possibilities

Near Berlin, Tad told me, there is a big lake with a beach. The heads of the German Reich were living in the vicinity. Hitler, Himmler and others had summer houses by the lake. I remember my mother telling me that when the Germans took me in their arms, I would call them "Daddy." I wondered what we had been doing there. I also wondered what contacts my mother had and why others thought that she could change outcomes.

These questions became even more intriguing because shortly after being in Berlin, my mother and I were on a train going to Auschwitz. Since both sides of my family were involved in Resistance movements, I was curious about whether my mother also doing information searches and relating them to others. This is something that probably I will never know for certain. While I was still living at home, the war was never discussed, but sometimes I heard pieces of conversation about it when friends were visiting. It could be assumed that if my mother were in fact in the Resistance, she must have somehow lost her covert status and, as a result, we were sent to Auschwitz.

Chapter 3

MY FATHER, LEON NIRENBERGER

My father, Leon Nirenberger, was born on February 9, 1906, in Łodz, Poland. His parents, as far as I know, were well-off. His family came from a Jewish sect in Germany called *Ashkenaz*.

There is a story behind the Nirenberger name. When I was a boy, I was told that our name was Nirenberg without the "er" at the end. In fact my paternal grandfather's name was Nirenberg. My father added the "er" in the European tradition. For example, "Nuremberger" refers to a citizen of Nuremberg. When I was in France visiting my cousin Tad Nowicki, we came upon some official papers from Russia that showed the Nirenberg name written with a "y" instead of an "i." My cousin and I tried to find a reason why that should be. The best theory we could think of was that when a bureaucrat wrote the name, he used a quill and an ink well. When starting to write a "y," he started on the left with the first upper leg, then came down half way, then up to finish the second leg. Then he stroked down to finish. However, if the quill dried at the first leg, the letter ended up as an "i" instead of a "y."

My paternal grandfather was Lazar Nirenberg and my paternal grandmother was Felicia Dorfegajczow. My cousin Tad Nowicki told me that my grandfather had a book store and some textile interests.

My father had three other siblings: A brother, Joseph, and two sisters, Marisia and Cesia. Cesia and my grandmother were killed by Germans during World War II. Both were thrown from the second floor of their house. My Aunt Marisia became a well-known dress designer in Brazil.

My Uncle Joseph was born on August 13, 1896. He was ten years older than my father. I don't know when my grandfather died, but afterwards, Joseph took care of the family. He was responsible for my father's education. After my father finished school in Poland, my uncle sent him to the university in Nice, France. Nice at that time and still today is a tourist town as well as a university center.

When I was a young man, my father often told me about his experiences in Nice. I remember very well his story about a girlfriend of his. Her parents were not very happy that my father was seeing her. One day while they were together, the girl's parents chased him away with an umbrella.

I don't have any concrete information about what happened after my father returned to Poland, but I do know that my dad's family was multilingual. Besides Polish, my father could speak Russian, German, French and most of the Slavic tongues. However, he never learned English.

My parents met during a ski trip, which I have described in the chapter about my mother. They were married on March 7, 1938, in Chorzow, Poland. My mother often told that my father was very well-known in Warsaw. He was the first to own a Renault, which is a French car. Although he never held public office, my father was involved in decision-making and acted as a sounding board for politicians.

My father had a textile business in the best part of the town by the Vistule, a river that crosses the town and splits it in two. Now there is a four-tower apartment complex on the site of my father's business. Like everything else, his business was confiscated by the Germans during the war.

Several months after I was born, my father went to France to oversee his textile factories. When the war broke out, he was unable to return to Poland. Not long ago, my cousin Wiesia's husband, Dr. Adam Nowosławski, told me it was a very good omen that my father had not been allowed to return to Poland. He said that it probably saved his life. During the war, my father was sought by the Germans. After the war, he was sought by the Russians.

While he was in France early in the war, my father became part of the Polish Air Force. When I was a young boy, I knew that he was in the Polish Air Force. However, I was not sure in what capacity he served. At first, I had a notion that he sat behind the pilot and took pictures. Later when my wife Carolina and I went to France, my cousin Tad Nowicki told me that my father was a pilot. Tad received this information from his dad. Tad also told me that when he and his brother Oleg met my father for the first time, they were disappointed because he was a short-statured man and was not very muscular. They thought that pilots had to be tall, muscular men.

My father was part of a Polish Air Force squadron that participated in defending London during the 1940 London Blitz by Hitler's Lufthansa. There is a very interesting anecdote about the Polish pilots who were in London. At first, the English pilots did not want the Polish pilots to fly with them because of language difference. They also did not trust the Polish pilots' ability to fly. However, after several months of very heavy losses, the English brass decided to use the Polish pilots. In the end, the Polish squadron was recognized and decorated.

My father was shot down several times. The last time he was shot down, he walked to Switzerland. Much later in my life, I learned that he had two bank accounts in Switzerland from before the war. While in Switzerland, my father was taken to an internment camp where he was put to work building roads. He returned to France in 1945 when the war ended.

In France, he started to rebuild his business. The factories were still in Lyon, in the south of France. The offices in other countries were slowly rebuilt with the help of partners. One of his best friends and partners was a man named Josephson who lived in Sweden. Later, Mr. Josephson helped my father to get my mother and me out of Poland and safely into Sweden.

Chapter 4

I was born in Warsaw, Poland, on March 14, 1939, one year after my parents were married. My parents were well-to-do, so some might say that I was born with a silver spoon in my mouth. They named me Andrzej Lucian Nirenberger.

Five-and-a-half months later, World War II started. I was told we were living then in an up-scale part of Warsaw. My parents owned a very nice villa which was well known in town at that time.

My father had a textile business in Warsaw. He also had textile factories in France. He left Poland after my birth to visit his foreign offices. I did not see my father again until we were reunited eight years later in France. I was told that he had made an attempt to return to Poland. However, he was not able to do so.

I have a collage in my mind of the time that my mother and I were in Warsaw during the war. It might not be in chronological order, but the memories are very real.

There were only two modes of public transportation in Warsaw: tram-ways and wagons. Tramways were often stopped on the track and taken over by the Germans when they needed to go somewhere. Each time, the Germans forced us to leave the tramway. Horse-drawn wagons were used by most of the Jews and sympathizers. Each wagon was mostly made of wood and had wooden wheels. Inside, there were wooden benches on each side. We would get in through two or three wooden steps located in the back.

I remember enjoying the rides. I have a vivid image of the horse's rump going left, right, left, right, in cadence with his hooves. I was fascinated by the driver's skill. With just the tone of his voice, he could make the horse go or stop. At that time the hostile environment was not my concern. I just relished the moment. Now, every time that I see a pick-up truck with wooden sides or anything comparable, I recall the smell and the ambiance of that time. It is hard to explain, but I can feel it in my throat.

When the Germans invaded Poland, our villa was the first house they requisitioned for their use. From that moment, my mother and I were at the mercy of everyone. We stayed with friends as long as we could, until they themselves were displaced from their homes.

For a time, my maternal grandmother helped us by selling coffee and hot tea from two big baskets that she carried on her arms. Besides the tea and coffee, she smuggled eggs, meat, and other items that she sold on the street. Under the German occupation, this black market was against the law. My grandmother took a very big risk every day just to survive and to help us. Most of the time, if people were caught smuggling, they would be hanged or shot.

When my grandmother was unable to help us with food, my mother looked for pieces of coal on railroad tracks. We had a stove that heated our room when we had coal. My mom cooked some pig's fat that she cut in little squares on top of the stove when we had coal. The fat was all we had to eat for the day. In Polish, fat prepared that way is called *skfarki*.

I remember one day when I wanted something, my mother indicated that she did not have any money. Very casually, I told her to go to the bank.

At one time, we were living in a several-stories-tall building. My mother and I slept in one room. When Warsaw was being bombed, we went to the bomb shelter located in the basement of the building. That happened several times each night.

During one bombing, I broke my right arm. While my mom and I were running towards the shelter, a bomb fell too close to me. Suddenly, instead of running, I was flying because the vacuum followed by the surge of air lifted me from the ground and threw me down the shelter stairs and up against a wall. My arm was in plaster for a short time, when the same thing happened again — same flying through the air, same bomb shelter, same wall.

During another bombing, we were in a shelter with a lot of other people. Later on, I was told by my mother that most of those people were relatives and friends. A bomb came through the chimney and exploded inside the shelter. Everybody, except my mother and me, was killed.

Finally, my mother told me that we were not going to rush to the bomb shelter anymore. She decided that if God wanted us to die, it would happen no matter where we were.

My mother had friends who sometimes permitted us to have shelter for the night, even though we had to move almost every night. Because we had to march most of the time to get out of harm's way, my mother and I often slept in barns where hay was a luxury. We also slept in forests under the brushes. At one time, my hair was completely shaved off because I had lice. However, that was not an uncommon situation. Most of the children had their heads shaved for the same reason. When the nights were cold, we slept back-to-back to keep ourselves warm.

I remember lying in a trench and looking up at the night sky. I could see the flares that the German aviators were dropping to target the bombing sites. My mother and I were saturated with light as the planes flew over us. I could hear the whistling and then the swooshing of the bombs as they fell near us.

Another time, while my mother and I were in a field, an airplane flying very low tried to shoot and kill us. My mother and I dove to the ground and the plane missed us. My mother later told me that it was a *Trikotka*, a double-winged airplane which had three engines.

Since we did not have a regular place to stay during most of the war, there were times when we marched in long columns with many other displaced people. We did not go to any specific place. We just fled from either the Germans or the Russians. The direction of the march was set by whoever was winning at the time.

I remember walking with my mother on sidewalks filled with people lying on the pavement. Some were dead; some were barely moving. I recall stepping over them. Somehow, I did not ask my mother why they were there. It seemed that I knew.

One night, we were walking very silently on a dark street. There were two faint street lights on each end of the block. A German Army truck with the lights on was parked on the same side of the street where we were walking. My mother told me to be very quiet and to walk behind her very close to the building walls. When we were near the truck, there were some steps on the left. At the top of the steps was a door that my mother started to scratch. After a short time, the door opened and we went in. My memory stops suddenly when that door opened. To this day, I still don't know how the Germans in the truck did not see us.

One day my mother and I decided to visit my cousin Wiesia Nowosławska. I called Wiesia my cousin in the European manner of calling close friends and their offspring our uncles, aunts, and cousins, although they were not blood relatives. Wiesia was sixteen years old then and was part of the Polish Underground. While we were walking along the sidewalk, my mother suddenly told me to walk silently. "No talking," she said. "Look in front of you." But I could not miss seeing what was happening. As we approached, I remember seeing a house with four or five cement stairs on my left. On the top step were two men in Gestapo uniforms. Their boots were shiny and their uniforms were very impressive to a child. We passed by my cousin without looking in her direction. I learned later that the Gestapo was there to arrest her. Wiesia was interned in Auschwitz and in two other concentration camps, Majdanek and Ravensbruck.

By the end of the war, most of Poland was under the Russian Army's control. We were living in a suburb of Warsaw then. It was not our own place, but it provided a moment of respite after moving all the time. I know now that we were still hiding. We lived in a group of wooden houses among tall trees, along with several families who had young children. Our house had a veranda.

One day Wiesia arrived on foot. I was told that she walked for over a week to the place where we lived. Now that I think of it, she must have somehow discovered where we were staying. What impressed me most was Wiesia's backpack. The brown leather backpack was square and had straps that were doubled but very narrow. To me, the most interesting part was the flap which served as the cover. It was made of a different type of leather and looked like cow's hair combed from top to bottom. The color was a very light yellowish brown on top that faded to a pure white towards the bottom. I don't know why, but to this day, I can still see Wiesia's backpack in front of me.

My mother was a very strong woman, mentally as well as physically. There was a water well at the place we were living. What happened next was still another survival act performed by my mother. Since the Russian soldiers were everywhere, many women were taken advantage of. One day while my mother was outside close to the well, a Russian soldier was bothering her. Before he knew what was happening, he found himself falling down into the well. If I remember correctly, no one came to his help. I think he might have drowned.

Eventually, my mother and I went into Warsaw to try to leave Poland. We had the necessary papers for the Germans to identify us. My mother's passport had both our photographs in addition to loose documents which were needed to prove where we were living. However, we were not living where those papers showed. My mother's identification papers included the German stamp produced for Polish consumption that included the price in Polish *zlotys* as well as Hitler's Nazi emblem, the swastika.

By then the Russian Army controlled all of Warsaw. I am not sure of the exact date, but just before the Iron Curtain fell, we departed from Poland on a Swedish diplomatic plane. Later I learned that we had falsely passed as Swedish embassy staff. My father, through his contacts, had organized everything

I remember that when we marched toward the plane, there was barbwire on both sides of the entrance to the very small runway. There were two Russians on each side with small machine guns hanging from their shoulders and resting against their bodies. The Russians had round, fur hats and long, heavy grey overcoats with very large fur collars.

My mother told me to walk in silence and close to her. She warned me not to look at them. While we walked, she kept repeating, "Look in front of you. Look in front of you." We did not have any suitcases. Whatever we had on our backs was our luggage.

My mother and I flew to Stockholm, Sweden, where a new era in my life began.

Chapter 5

My mother and I arrived in Sweden on December 7, 1945. The only things that we had with us were what we had on our backs. It was cold and snow was everywhere. We were welcomed by Mr. and Mrs. Josephson, who were partners with my father in the textile business. This was the first time I had been in a big town without being bombed. Everything seemed to be very peaceful. For the first time in my life, I had a ride in a car. I thought it was fantastic.

The Josephsons were very helpful. They came with warm coats for us. When we went to their home in Stockholm, life was so different for me. There were sheets and no fear of bombs. Without any problems, I learned Swedish, and within three months, I was fluent. I don't remember how long we stayed in their house, but I was awed by everything.

They had tablecloths and they used crystal at the dinner table. The food was good and plentiful. I remember that when we were at the table ready to eat, there were two big pitchers of milk. During our stay in Stockholm, I drank so much milk that to this day, I do not drink any. Neither do I use butter. Everybody had a little dish on the right side for the butter. The butter looked like a little ball with a design on it. Later on, I saw how the balls were made. The maid took butter from a package and rolled it between two flat, spoon-like utensils. She rolled it for a while and it turned into a nice ball of butter with a design on it. I thought it was great.

To this day, I remember the joys of having toys and being able to be a kid. At the Josephsons I received my first-ever toy. It was a Walt Disney Pluto dog on a wooden square block. When I pushed under the block with my fingers, Pluto moved in all directions. My second toy was a little car that I played with from room to room. The car was a beautiful British racing green and to this day it is my preferred color. Every time I see this color, it reminds me of that time. I remember when I was on my knees pushing the small car and making the engine noise with my mouth, my mother would tell me not to make such noise because the cars were silent. She probably was tired of hearing me.

I also received new warm clothes since it was winter and cold outside. A little later on, I received my first skis. I had no problems to learn how to ski. Within a week, I could ski with anybody. The Josephsons and their son Bob and my mother and I went cross country skiing in the forest. One time when I went skiing with Bob, I came back at the end of the day and was told that my ears were frostbitten. At that time I did not know what it meant. To this day, when the weather is cool, my ears tingle.

After living with the Josephsons for a short time, we went to live in Skorbe, a locality about twenty kilometers from Stockholm. As I remember it, the main house was a huge building, several stories high. In front there was a big circle with a lot of snow and a paved road going around it. On each side of that big house there were two other much smaller houses at about forty-five degree angles. Later on I realized that the help was living there.

When I entered the big house through the main door, there was a large, curved stairway. The end of the stairway opened to a huge, grand-entrance room. On one side there was a dining room where all three meals were served. I believe that this building was a pension where a lot of refugees were staying.

In Skorbe I celebrated Christmas for the first time. At least it was the first time that I was cognizant of it. At Christmas time, everything was decorated. Just like on a post card, there was a sleigh pulled by horses. Inside the main house a huge, articulated Santa Claus hung from the top of the banister. When I came down the stairs, I pulled the string hanging from the Santa Claus and he moved his arms and legs. This was something new for me and I remember playing with it for a long time.

For me, this first Christmas was like a fairy tale. There was no end to the gifts. I received a leather ski outfit that included a hat and gloves in addition to the jacket and the pants. I also received my second pair of skiis.

Our first winter of freedom passed having fun cross-country skiing, going to school, making snowmen, and having snowball fights. It was a fabulous time in my life. It was great fun for me to be able to do most anything I wanted. I even skied in forests with skiers who were mostly adults.

The main road was about one kilometer from the big house. To go to school, I needed to get to the main road so I could take the bus. During the winter I had fun because I skied to the main road and waited for the bus. I remember that when cars passed by, their tires made a certain whistling noise. When I hear that noise now, it reminds me of solitude and quiet feelings.

Because the war was no longer central to our lives, I had a very good time with my mother. I think that in Sweden, without my knowing it at the time, she became my best friend. We had time to bond and to do things together without fear.

When winter slowly went away, spring came and a whole new recreational life started for me. My mom and I went often into the nearby forests. My mother was known for finding wild blueberries, wild raspberries, and mushrooms. I learned to recognize the good mushrooms from the poisonous ones.

We often looked for wild blueberries, and this was the first time I was introduced to them. I always ate more than I put in the basket. We brought the blueberries to the big house where everybody was waiting for them. To this day, I love blueberries.

We also looked for wild flowers. We found small, stemmed blue flowers that grew all together and looked like a carpet. I don't know their name, but they were beautiful. We also found tall, stemmed yellow flowers. I don't know their name in Swedish, but in French they are called *jonquilles*.

These walks through the forest with my mother were beautiful. We were the only two people, she and I. It was serene and quiet among the tall trees. I discovered moss and dirt by-ways. I had the time to see tree leaves and hear the birds. For the first time, I also saw wild animals. My mother and I saw bears from a safe distance.

My mother also taught me how to dance. In Skorbe, we often enjoyed dances, as well as amateur theater. I remember participating in plays but I don't remember what roles I played. Sometimes the Josephsons came visit us and took us for rides in their car. They also took us to their home.

There were two young girls working at the pension. I do not remember their names, but I remember how nice they were. They played with me and helped me in many, many ways. They taught me how to wax skis. They showed me how and when to use the right wax for the right kind of snow.

Later, I learned how to ride a bicycle. I did not take the easy way. I learned how to ride on a man's bicycle. Because I was small, I had to ride with my body to one side and under the upper bar. One of the girls helped me. She held the saddle and told me to pedal. After a while, I looked behind me and found that no one was holding me. From then on I was fine, but naïve. I don't remember who told me that if I let the air out of the tires, I would have a smoother ride. For a long time I rode with two flat tires. One day I was told to stop doing that. I remember that I got scared because I felt I had done wrong, so I ran away, leaving the bicycle on the ground.

My mother had lots of friends in Skorbe. Most of them were refugees from the war in Poland. One of her best friends was Bronia Rosenbaum, who was Jewish and was like part of the family to me. Bronia left Sweden after we did. She went to Israel, got married, and had a son. My mother kept contact with her throughout her life.

After all that wonderful time, there was talk about my mom and me traveling to Switzerland, but my mother did not tell me why. I knew that Sweden would soon become a memory. To this day it is the most beautiful memory that I cherish.

Chapter 6

My mother and I left Sweden for Bienne, which is located in the German part of Switzerland. People from the French side call it Berne. Bienne was a very nice city. On the main thoroughfare there was a big, deep pit where black bears were on display like in a zoo. This was something very unusual for me. I had seen bears in Sweden from a safe distance, so it was exciting to see them so closely. For the first time in my life, I saw mountains and cows with big bells around their necks. The food in Bienne was very similar to Swedish food.

I learned German and once again it did not take me long to speak fluently. I loved to learn languages. Even at that young age I was fascinated at being able to speak in different tongues.

Boarding school in Lausanne was fun. I enjoyed being with other kids. The education was good and that is why my parents sent me there. All the teachers were priests. The nuns did the women's jobs.

We went to Mass every day and I particularly hated Sunday Mass. The Mass was in Latin, so in my mind the priest could be saying whatever he wanted. The Sunday Mass was all right at the beginning. Then we had to kneel and the priest lit the incense. When he blessed the altar and the people in the church with the incense, it was time for me to faint. Every Sunday I fainted on cue. To this day, I do not like the smell of incense.

I had an serious question for the priests, but they never gave me a satisfactory answer. Keep in mind that I was very young and in a Catholic boarding school. Since I was taught that only Catholics could go to Heaven, I wanted to know what happened to the Jews, especially since my father was Jewish. The standard answer was that I must have faith. Today the question is not important, but it haunted me for a long time.

I remember a few instances when I was not at my best. As kids, we always tried to make bedtime interesting. We slept in a large dormitory room and about twelve to fifteen of us gave the priests a hard time. One night some of us decided that we would sleep with our heads at the foot of the beds. At the time there was no priest in the dormitory, but they usually passed by to see if we were behaving. It did not take long before I was flying from my bed over two others, then landing on the third bed half way on the floor. The priest I had not seen coming slapped me on the side of the neck. That was the last time that I tried to make things interesting.

Another time, we were going to have an exam the next morning and I was not prepared. I do not remember now what the exam was about, but I recall deciding to moan and groan all night long about one of my knees. The next day I said that I did not feel good. The nun came and took my temperature and to my surprise I did not have to take the exam.

Everything was not bad. We had good times playing. We also went to see the large ferry boats on Lake Geneva, which the French called Lac Leman. When I was researching my first stay in Switzerland, I found a letter and a picture from a very young girl who was interested in a certain eight-year-old boy. Her name was Josette and she was no more than nine years old. Interestingly, I do not remember her, but maybe that was because I hadn't started to notice girls yet.

About six months after arriving in Switzerland, I discovered that we were moving once again. My mother and I were finally going to be reunited with my father in France.

Chapter 7

When we left Switzerland, my mom and I traveled to France. For the first time since I was a baby, I was going to meet my dad. I really do not remember how I was feeling at the time. I don't even remember arriving in France. It should have been a very important day for me, but somehow I have a complete blank.

The next thing I remember is being with my father in a bank. It was very busy and I could hear people talking. I suddenly realized that they were talking a language that I could not understand. I also remember that my first impression was that all those people were talking in a baby language.

My parents and I lived in a hotel. I don't know its name, but it was on a busy Paris street. This was a very different time in my life. I did not know how to handle it. Everything was so new and different. My mom had someone else and I was not sure of anything. I know that for at least two years I called my father "Sir." It was always, "Yes, Sir," or "No, Sir."

After a short time, we moved to Vigneux, a village about twelve miles from Paris. It was just after the war and it was difficult to find any housing or land to buy. My father had to rebuild his textile business and take care of his family at the same time.

We moved into a very small house. It had one bedroom, another room that was used for sleeping and for meals, and a small kitchen. On the side opposite the kitchen was a storage room that we entered from the outside. This is where we kept coal for the winter. We had no bathroom, shower, or any facility for grooming. When we wanted to go to the bathroom, we had to go outside to the outhouse. Every so often, I saw my dad emptying the outhouse.

I slept in the bedroom and when it rained, I had to have an umbrella above the bed because the roof leaked. There was one door from the kitchen to the outside. However, the door could not be opened. I do not remember why, but when we needed to go to the outhouse, we jumped through the kitchen window to get outside.

To the kitchen from the second room, there was a step the width of the door. I used this step often when I played conductor of the Paris Metro. I stepped on and off the kitchen step pretending that I was opening and closing the Metro's door. I was always fascinated by the conductor's uniform. I decided that when I grew up, I would be a conductor. When I rode the Metro, which was the Paris subway, and the controller came to punch the ticket, I could see myself in that uniform. Around that time, I saw some Boy Scouts and I liked their uniforms too, so I decided that I also wanted to be a Boy Scout. I talked with my parents about it and it seemed to me that I was going to join the Boy Scouts.

Our little house had a huge front yard with a water well. The well was not used, but it had water and a hand pump in working order. There was an oval lawn on the left side of the house. The pathway from the front door to the street was in the center of the front yard. On both sides of the pathway, we had bushes that flowered at certain times of the year. On the right side of the house, the yard looked like a jungle with all types of trees and bushes. At the end of the front yard there was a half wall with a grille that needed to be painted on top.

We had a big hazelnut tree at the end of the front yard. This tree was my favorite place to fly away to my dream land. I would climb the tree to a branch that looked like a seat. Actually, it was comfortable and I would imagine that I was in my airplane flying to distant, wonderful lands. When I was there, it was my time. No one could come and I did not want to share with anyone.

Coming to France was not anything like arriving in Sweden. For many years I had difficulties, although French, like other languages I encountered, was relatively easy for me. After a very short time, I was fluent in French. I went to the public school in Vigneux. I remember walking to school every day, which was fun for me. However, I was not happy in school and my performance was not very good, so I stayed only six months.

My dad had big responsibilities, especially for his business and his family. He also helped a lot of his friends whom he knew from Poland and some whom he had met in Switzerland and France. So, after my difficulties in the public school, it was decided that one of his friends, a lawyer and a professional translator who could not practice in France at the time, would become my tutor and help me to get up to par education-ally. His name was Raymond Lette.

This relationship was the best thing that happened to me. Mr. Lette taught me French grammar and opened doors to this special part of my childhood. I not only received a scholastic education, but I also explored art, life, history, and music. My father was instrumental in immersing me in classical music. We also went to classical concerts.

Some mornings started with my reading French or writing a *dictée*. Mr. Lette read and I wrote what he dictated. Afterwards, he showed me how many mistakes I had made. He explained the errors so I could understand the grammar or Latin roots of the words. In the beginning, I was not very good at it. It is much easier to speak a foreign tongue than to write it. Reading was not a problem.

On other days, my tutor and I did math. That was not difficult since language was not involved. We also watched movies. Some were funny movies of the Three Stooges type. Others were educational. Mr. Lette and I played soccer, a European form of football, on the front lawn. That was great fun for me. At the time I liked to play goal keeper because I liked to dive on the grass and stop the ball. On weekends, Mr. Lette, his wife, and their small child came to our house to have dinner with us.

Mr. Lette and I often went to Paris to visit museums. We sometimes explored one museum in a day. The Louvre or other such museums could take weeks. My tutor explained the purpose of each museum. To this day I remember a statue of an African woman in the Museum of Natural History. This statue fascinated me because it was not like any other. The woman's derrière protruded to such an extent that it looked like a seat. It was the first time in my life that I had seen a representation of a person of another color. We visited this museum many times. It was a complete new world for me.

I learned most of my French history by visiting the Museum of French History. I remember, in particular, the assassination of Marat, an important person in the French Revolution. Marat was assassinated while taking a bath. The museum did a wonderful job on that subject. When I arrived at the scene, the whole room was completely dark and the light shone only on the white bathtub and Marat's whitish body with the bleeding wound in his side. It was very scary because I didn't anticipate the vignette at that moment.

Mr. Lette and I also went to mosques, cathedrals, churches, and temples. I especially remember that when we were in a mosque, we had very strong tea or coffee in very small porcelain cups and very small round cookies. Inside the mosque, the colors were beautiful. Yellow, blue, and orange were mixed in different mosaic shapes. We also visited all the famous monuments in Paris. The tutoring lasted for one year. Because of Mr. Lette, I received the best education anyone could hope for.

Life was quiet and good, but it still did not feel like life in Sweden. However, I knew that I was safe and my mom was still close. It was a new world which I enjoyed. As a result, I no longer thought about that man who shared my mom, but who did not yet feel like my dad. For me it was an impasse.

During the time that I was tutored, I helped in the house. I went with my mom to the stores to buy food and other things that we needed. Shopping in France is not like shopping in the United States. For bread, we went to the bakery. For milk, cheese, and other items including wine, we went to the dairy store. I remember on one occasion I was sent to buy bread. My dad told me what to say in French: *un pain, s'il-vous-plais.* I left for the bakery repeating that phrase all the way, but when I arrived, I did not know what I was saying. So instead of pointing to the bread and paying for it, I decided to walk back home without it. That happened at the very beginning when I did not know French well.

I remember another story that seemed very funny to me at the time. My dad and I went to shop in Vigneux. He bought several bottles of mineral water and some eggs. At that time, we shopped with net sacks called *filets* in French. While walking home, my dad decided to swing the *filet* over his shoulder, but he completely forgot about the eggs. Soon, the eggs were dripping down his suit coat and I could not stop laughing. I did not tell him until we arrived home and my mom also started to laugh. Because my dad did not get mad, I think that for the first time I felt closer to him.

My young boy's life was mostly quiet and normal. Things seemed to be going along pretty well. However, my parents discovered that I was not doing too well psychologically. On July 14, France celebrates Bastille Day, which commemorates the freeing of political prisoners and others from the Bastille. To celebrate, all the towns and villages had fireworks. Every time a firework was launched, it made a lot of noise. When I heard the firework explosions, I became hysterical. I cried and screamed and went to hide under my iron bed. There was nothing that my parents could do to convince me I was safe. It was the beginning of a very rough time for me. That difficult time lasted well beyond my teenage years. One side effect lasted until my middle thirties.

Looking back, I think I was probably suffering from Post Traumatic Stress Disorder (PTSD). However, at that time people were not yet familiar with PTSD. I do not remember seeing a psychiatrist since that was usually reserved for severely mentally ill people, not children hiding under their beds during fireworks. During my young years, seeing a psychiatrist was also considered a stigma by families of certain social levels.

My parents did what they thought was best for me at the time. Since there was nothing available psychologically, their solution was to try solving my problem through education. Therefore, I had to have the best in their eyes. They decided to send me to the Ecole des Roches which is still considered the best and most well-known boarding school in France. The school, which was founded in 1899, was composed of several parts --- primary, college, and baccalaureate levels. Each group was separate from the others and students came from many countries.

While my parents were busy selecting the best boarding school for me, I was still dreaming about becoming a Boy Scout. Looking back, however, I am glad that getting a good education took precedence.

Chapter 8

THE WRONG UNIFORM!

I was fascinated by uniforms when I was growing up. I wanted to become a Boy Scout and I remember believing that my parents agreed with me. However, maybe I misunderstood them because I ended up in boarding school instead. My parents told me that I needed to pass a test. Since I was fixated on joining the Boy Scouts, I was convinced the test was for acceptance into that group.

When my parents and I arrived at a school, we were guided to a classroom which was very bright with sun shining through four or five windows. At one end of the room was the usual teacher's desk on top of a wooden platform with its own step. The platform looked worn from all the walking the teacher must have done. The dreaded blackboard was behind the teacher's desk. The wooden pupils' desks were all in one piece, including the slanted desk top with a quill, a pen holder, and an ink well, plus a bench for each pupil.

One person from the school, my parents, and I were the only ones in the classroom that day. I did not know who the person from the school was, but I assumed he was a teacher. I was asked if I were comfortable and then the teacher explained to me that he was going to ask me some questions that I would answer by writing on the blackboard.

I was about ten years old and the whole experience seemed to last a long time. I was asked to write things which I don't remember now. I know I had to solve problems and to show on the blackboard how I arrived at the solutions. If I remember correctly, I had no difficulties answering all the questions. Actually, I was told during the session that I was very good. Next, I was asked to answer questions orally, including math, French grammar, and other subjects. When all the testing was finished, I was told that I was going to be accepted.

I was very happy and I could see myself in a Boy Scout uniform. However, it did not work out that way. While we were driving home, my parents told that I was going to go to a school where I would stay and not come home at the end of the day. I still thought that the school in question was where all the Boy Scouts were going. No matter what my parents told me, I related everything to the Boy Scout idea.

When we arrived home, I was told that I was going to live at the school and that it was going to be my home. They said that if I were doing well in school, they would visit me when permitted. I did not know what to make of all that news. I had never been in a school so far away, so when my parents explained that I would wear a uniform, I still thought that it had something to do with Boy Scouts.

The preparation for my new life was not very exciting to me. I knew I would be going into an area I had never experienced. I received all the necessary materials. I vividly remember the small, wooden box for my quill, pencils, and eraser. The lid, which slid off, was adorned with flowers. It took several days to prepare me for my new life.

École des Roches was certainly not a neighborhood school. I needed to take the train to the boys' school in Verneuille sur Havre in Savoie, which is in the northeastern part of France close to the mountains. This was the first time I would be traveling without my mom. When we arrived at the train station, we discovered a lot of other parents with their children. Everyone met the chaperones who were going to be with us during the trip. The scene in the first Harry Potter movie, where Harry is taking the train to Hogwarts, reminded me of my trip. It was very much the same way, except that I did not have to pass through a stone pillar to reach the train.

I do not remember crying when the train started. I was with other boys and I did not have any difficulty becoming friends with them. We acted as if we had known each other forever. Perhaps it was the lonely feeling at the time that made us feel close to each other. Six boys traveled in each train compartment and our suitcases were stored above our heads. The trip took a long time. The train was pulled by a steam engine and during the night I remember that I was almost hypnotized by the cadence of the wheels on the rails.

At night the whole compartment was quiet. When I was not sleeping, the noise of the train was a comfort to me since it took my mind off the separation from my parents. The separation was mostly from my mom, since at that time I still addressed my dad as, "Yes, Sir," or "No, Sir." I must have finally fallen asleep because when I opened my eyes, one of the chaperones was checking that all was well. At the same time, he gave us small cakes for breakfast. Not much of a breakfast, but better than nothing.

When we arrived at our destination, a bus was waiting to take us to the school. At this time, the atmosphere was festive. I probably felt like many of the others that a new life was around the corner and that there was no going back. The bus took us to the school, and to my surprise the entrance to the ground was absolutely beautiful. It was like entering an enchanted forest. Huge trees lined both sides of the road. The tops of the trees touched to make a grand arch. It was absolutely gorgeous. To this day, when I drive through a similar roadway, I am reminded of arriving at school that first day.

When we reached our destination, we were split into groups and told that a teacher would take us to our living quarters. I was going to live with my music teacher. This was really nice because it did not look like a school dormitory or a military camp. From the outside, it looked like a normal, two-story house. Inside, it was very comfortable. The first floor held a dining room, a large kitchen, and a room for music stands and musical instruments, including a piano. On the second floor, we found two simply-furnished bedrooms. There were three single iron beds in each room, with thin mattresses, sheets, and two blankets. The large window had a view of a square lawn. We each had an armoire for our clothes and other items. We also had a place for special things like cookies or other goodies that our parents gave us.

The rest of that day, we were introduced to rules and regulations and schedules for all the meals and classes. We received our uniforms, which consisted of pants and shorts, along with a jacket and a blazer. We had to furnish white, blue and grey shirts with both short and long sleeves. The shoes that we brought from home were either black or dark brown.

Six students lived with the music teacher. I do not remember his name, but he was married and had two grown children, a boy and a girl, who also were musicians. I found out later that the whole family played music. When I had my first meal with them, I have to say it was not bad. It was very much like being in a big family. All of us sat at the table with the family while two people served the meal. Lunch and dinner were very French. It took about one hour for the lunch and longer for dinner.

The table was very sophisticated with a tablecloth, china, and a vase with flowers. For me, it had a feeling of home.

At night we had to be in bed by nine, with lights out by 9:30. That first night when we went to bed, everyone was kind of sad. The realization had just hit — we were alone, our parents were not with us, and they would not be for an uncertain period of time. Without words, we were aware of how we felt, but perhaps we did not want the others to know.

That night, I went to bed and when the lights were turned off, after some silent moments, I started to cry. I put my head under the covers so that no one could hear me. This was the start of my first experience with boarding school.

The next day school started.

Chapter 9

The first morning of boarding school, I opened my eyes and was not sure where I was. For an instant that seemed like an eternity, I did not know what to do. I did not even realize that I was not alone, although three of us slept in the same room. I did not even notice the sounds of classical music coming from downstairs. Then it suddenly hit me. I was at École des Roches, starting my new life with a lot of other boys who were also feeling alone.

Everything seemed to be moving in slow motion. I knew I had to start getting ready, but I wanted to know about everything that was happening before I made my first move. I realized then that the music was not coming from a radio, but rather from someone playing. Suddenly, a woman in a black dress and a white apron came into the room and rushed us to get ready for breakfast. She said we had half an hour to get ready, and I was. We had two roomy bathrooms where several of us could brush our teeth and do what we needed. We were given a choice of what we wanted to wear. That is, we could choose between long pants or shorts, and between long-sleeved shirts or short-sleeved shirts. It really did not make much difference, since the pants were grey or dark blue and the shirts were grey. We also had two dark blue blazers. However, even this small liberty to choose let me feel good to be in control.

The stairs from our room made a ninety-degree turn to the left and ended in the dining room. The music room was on the right side of the stairway. The music teacher, his wife, and his two grown children were playing a Beethoven piece. I soon discovered that the family played the same piece each morning. The lady of the house played the piano, her husband played the cello, and their children played violin and viola. When the six of us were seated at the table, the four musicians came to sit with us. Later, I learned that they were all teachers at the school.

The breakfast was not what I expected. Everything was so new to me. We were served porridge, which had never been in my diet. I did not like it and I did not like the fact that it had milk in it. By that time, I had stopped drinking milk because I drank so much of it in Sweden. In addition to the porridge, we had pieces of bread with jelly. Of course, I did not have any choice, so I had to develop a taste for that thing called porridge. To this day, I do not eat that concoction. Even now, when I hear that Beethoven piece, I have the taste of porridge in my mouth.

During meals, there was no talking until dessert. At breakfast time, there was no time for any talk. We were told by the head of the house that starting the next day, all of us would go to a daily Mass and to our classes. We also learned that our parents' visitations were not a sure thing. If my work was mediocre or not presented well, my parents were not able to visit me for the next two weeks.

Most of the time, each day was about the same. The buildings were so far apart, we had to ride from our base to the classrooms. At noon we had lunch and then a one-hour nap. After the nap, we had sports until four o'clock. Then we had *quatre heures*, a time when we had a break for something light to eat and drink. We ate a *pain au chocolat*, a piece of sweet bread with chocolate, or regular bread with a piece of chocolate. After that, we went back to school until six thirty. When school was finished, all the students went back to their respective houses.

I do not remember exactly what I did on my first day in the classroom. However, I remember that discipline was very strict. We were not allowed to sit at our desks until the teacher came into the room and told us to sit down. Obviously, there was no talking. We had a woman for teacher. École des Roches was a Catholic school and the teaching faculty was a mixture of priests and laity.

My life at the school was busy and very interesting. We had *solfeggio* which I liked very much. In that class, I learned the scales and I also learned how to sing those scales. I had piano lessons each day, along with piano practice. Of course, I also studied all the basic French courses in arithmetic, French, and the other elementary-grade classes.

Besides the academic classes, I took sculpting, which was not my favorite pastime. Actually, I was very bad at it and I asked to be excused from the class. However, that was in vain. But I did learn other crafts. I still have a coaster that I made, dated "Christmas 1947." The base of the coaster is a thick blue carton with eleven slots toward the center of the base. The slots are shaped in such a way that a circle is formed. Through those slots, I wove different colors of yarn. My coaster has three colors: yellow, which is the main color, along with green and red.

In the evenings, we had until 7:30 for homework. When I had trouble with it, the master of the house helped me, just as parents do home. At eight o'clock we had dinner. None of us young people could talk until dessert was served. Then the talk was about school, music, and anything else that had to do with school. By nine, I was in my room, and at 9:30, the lights were out. Sometimes, after lights-out, we tried to read under the sheets with flashlights. However, if any one of us got caught, we were all punished.

It was a surprise for everyone, including me, to find out that I was a sleep-walker. Not only I was a sleep-walker, but I also screamed during the process. In some instances, I woke up for a second, realized what was happening, then fell back to sleep instantly. But one time I remember walking down the stairs. At the bottom, I woke up just long enough to tell myself, "You are doing it again!" Then I fell back to sleep. I did not remember anything about that night, except the part when I woke up. Later on, I was told that I walked around the dining table, then up the stairs and back into my bed.

In another instance, when I was sleep-walking, I opened the window and stepped out. Unfortunately, I was on the second floor and I fell onto the lawn. No one was aware of what had happened until the next morning when I woke up. I remember I had my eyes closed and I felt wet and cool. When I opened my eyes, I realized that I was lying on the grass and the dew was all over me and the grass. I had a tough time getting back into the house because it was still before the wake-up call and it took a long time for someone to open the door. Afterwards, the window was locked in such a way that I could not open it again.

My parents were notified and I was sent to many doctors, but I do not remember seeing a psychiatrist. My medication was mostly in the form of syrup taken several times a day. If one syrup did not work, I was given another. I also took prescribed pills. Everyone who was responsible for me made sure that the medications were taken on a regular basis. However, I continued to sleep-walk and scream most nights. This condition lasted for a very long time and it was only one of many symptoms that continued to surface.

Much later, I found some letters the school master sent to my father about my condition. He said that after my parents came to visit me, I would sleep much better, scream less, and be much less agitated. He also indicated to my father that no one should make me feel more important than anyone else. The master felt that possibly I could feel special because of all the attention I was getting during my hard time. He said that I would not receive any special consideration and I would be treated like everyone else.

As I look back, I wonder how much of all this was related to the flash-backs to the bombings and how much was a result of the separation from my mother. But at the age I was, I did not ask any questions. Sadly, Post Traumatic Stress Disorder (PTSD) had not yet been identified, so treatments available today were unknown then.

Not everything was bad at school. At École des Roches I started to play tennis. It was not a very brilliant start. I missed the first ball that was played towards me and it hit me in the right eye. I had a nice shiner for a while. Since that time, I continued to play tennis and after several years, I became good at it.

I also was introduced to softball and I played in two or three games. I remember one game particularly where I was batting. I was told to try for *tombeau ouvert*, which in French means to run like hell if I hit the ball. Unfortunately, I was thrown out at first base. After that I never played the game again since I did not like it.

European soccer, which is a form of football, was my game. Getting to the football field was a nice walk. I had to cross a very small wooden bridge that lay across a creek bordered by huge trees. The football field was a cow pasture with goals on each end. There were no markings on the field and we just played for the fun of it. We were careful to avoid the cow patties, which, it seemed, were our opposition.

I also participated in the track and field events. The whole course was in a forest that belonged to the school. I remember that during the season I had jaundice and was sent to the school infirmary. I was admitted and confined and told to lie in bed until I got well. My parents were notified that I was sick, but they knew I was in good hands. The room was white with several beds, but I was the only one in the room. There was silence, the doors were closed, and I could hear voices in the distance. It was a very serene moment. The problem was that I was in bed on a Saturday when I was supposed to participate in a cross country race. So I decided to leave the infirmary and join the race.

It was the first time that I was running in that type of race. I remember I had to jump over fallen trees, water, and high obstacles. One particular obstacle made me stop and think about the rest of the race. I did not know if I wanted to continue. I had to jump from a retaining wall to a sand pit. From where I was standing, it seemed to be a long fall. However, the other participants were coming and I did not want to be considered a chicken, so I mustered all the courage that I had and I jumped. When I finished, I went back to the infirmary. I do not remember what place I finished, but I know that no one noticed that I had left my bed.

Another game that I discovered at the school was a flag game. I loved it. The game was played in the forest. We were split into two teams called Cowboys and Indians. The flags were behind our backs and the purpose was to take the flag from the opposition. This game would go on for several days. We hid in the forest and attacked in groups. When we lost our flags, we were considered dead. However, if we had other flags that we had won, we could use them and be alive again. It was a fantastic time for me. Every time that I found myself in a forest environment, I felt alive and happy. To this day, I love to be among trees and recall the excitement of that time.

I wrote to my parents quite often, not because I missed them as such, but because I wanted them to send me things. In general, the letters followed the same pattern.

"Dear Parents,

"I eat well, I play well, and I want you to send me a football, three tennis balls, my tennis racquet, and a care package."

Usually in the care package, I wanted *pain d'epice*, a French spice bread, some chocolate, and cookies. Sometimes my care packages contained oranges. After my "want" list was done, I asked my parents to come and visit me if my grades and behavior were up to par.

To my surprise, my parents saved many of my boarding school letters. Here is a translation of one of those letters:

"My Dear Parents,

"I thank you for the package and for the letter. I write on a simple piece of paper because I do not have any stationary. For shoes, I would like sandals if you can buy some. I would like the stationary with some lines. I hope that Claudie's little sister is well. I have a cold. Perhaps when you are here, I will feel better. I eat well and play well. I hope that you also are doing well. I would like to have my dictionary. Did my football arrive? Yes or no? Are Mr. and Mrs. Montaigu well? Is Mr. Montaigu's leg still hurting? I am writing you two pages and I will always write two pages. If my football arrived, please bring it. I thank you once more for the package. I would like some quills and a box for my quills. Goodbye and I'll see you Sunday.

"Mother and Father, kisses to both of you."

My parents had to take a plane or an overnight train to visit me. They came on Saturdays and usually left the next day. It was great to see them. However, to make the visit worthwhile for me, they had to bring me something. That sounds selfish now, but when I was a child, it was very important. When my parents came, we visited in the house where I lived. Then they gave me my care package and I showed them where I would keep it. After all the formalities, we went to eat in town.

After the first few months of my new life in boarding school, I became excited because Christmas was coming fast and I was getting ready to go home and see Claudie and Nono, my friends when I was not in school. When the time came for me to go home, my parents sent my train ticket. I took the trip home with the same students I had met when my boarding school life started. My parents waited for me at the station and my life was different again for a short time.

Chapter 10

Christmas was another change in my life, a change that I was happy to fully participate in. My parents were waiting for me at the train station in Paris. It was a very feverish time. All of us students were saying goodbye to each other and getting our suitcases. Our parents could not come onto the train to help us. By the time we finished getting off, I was happy to get some help with my luggage.

Vigneux is a suburb of Paris about twelve miles from the city. To get there by train, we had to go to the Gare de Lyon train station where we were given two choices. The Direct train only stopped at the bigger villages, while the Omnibus stopped at all the stations. People traveling by train to my village were very lucky because both trains stopped where I lived.

As a young boy, I loved to watch the steam engines come and go at the station. There was a special Pullman train that went from Paris all the way to Greece. I always wanted to take that train because it seemed so mysterious and exiting.

Vigneux had about 15,000 people, a plaza, and a lake. The lake was not what Americans think a lake should be. Instead, it was a very small lake where I fished for crawfish. In summer there were jousting competitions. We also had a bakery and a dairy where we could buy not only milk, but also wine. Our butcher shop was very popular. Another butcher shop sold horse meat, which was a delicacy in France. We had a cinema called the Bijou, which means *precious* in French. I felt very comfortable living in Vigneux. However, I never stayed long in any one place when I was a young boy.

At Christmas time, I was excited about playing with my friends Claudie and Nono again. Claudie was Harry and Mussia Zeimer's son. Harry Zeimer was my father's very good friend. My father helped him financially and tried to help him find a job in the engineering field. Mr. Zeimer used my room at home whenever he was working on a project. He closed the door and did not come out until he was finished. My mother and her lady cook prepared food for him and he ate in my room. Our cook was another person my family helped. After the war, it was hard to find work, so she came in each day to help my mother with the cooking and cleaning.

Claudie and I were very good friends. We were at each other's house all the time. The Zeimer's house was bigger than ours, but they were renting it. It was a two-story house with a curving staircase going to the second floor.

Nono Viale was the son of our neighbor. Both families were very friendly and I often played with their youngest son. Mr. Viale was well-known and well-liked in our community. He was a garbage collector for Vigneux and he also was a councilman for our little town. However, politically he was a Communist. My father was Jewish and a Capitalist. The situation reminds me of a very funny French movie called *Le Petit Monde de Don Camillo*. The movie told the story of a Communist mayor and a priest in a little farm village. Both men had different philosophies of life, but their lives were so intertwined that they could not do anything without having to compromise their values and everything else that was important for that little town.

It was great to see my friends again. I played football, a European form of soccer, on the street with Nono. We also played *billes*, marbles in English. I was not very good and lost all my *billes* in a very short time. Nono and I mostly played outside on the street, since there was no traffic, just houses on both sides. An older widow lived a few houses down. She had a black dog that never liked me. Every time that Nono and I went by the front yard, the dog got wild and showed his teeth.

I had a dog named Jikie. He was just a bastard, but we were friends. As much as I liked uniforms, my dog disliked them. Every time the water meter reader came, Jikie started barking and became very agitated. I indicated his behavior to my parents, but I was ignored. That was too bad, because one day a policeman came to our house and asked if the dog he had with him was ours. The problem was that policemen on bicycle patrol sometimes rode through our street. Jikie somehow escaped into the street and tore off one policeman's pant leg.

My father said the dog was not ours. However, I, lying sick in my bed, and said, "Yes, he's our dog." Of course, I embarrassed my father and we received a fine, but I don't remember how much. To redeem myself, I thought that I would remind my father that he told me to never lie. I don't recall what happened next, but it was an uncomfortable moment.

Christmas had not yet arrived, but Paris and the suburbs had some snow. Usually it did not snow, so I was surprised that Nono and I could build snowmen in my front yard. It was fun. We also had snowball fights. For a short time, it was almost was like Sweden.

Claudie and I mostly played in his house, since his house was bigger than ours and it was easier to play there. We had a game that we played when no one was at his home. We took an old wooden ironing board and we sat on it and went down the stairs from the second floor. It was fun and fast, just like luge on the snow. One day as we were going down, Claudie's mother Mussia came home and we met her just as we reached the end of our slope. Of course, that was our last descent and I was sent home where I was dealt with. A short time after being punished, we were again playing together.

Sometimes during my Christmas vacations, my family and I were invited to meet our neighbors two house down from ours. Their name was Montaigu and they had three children. The oldest boy was Jean Louis. Next came his sister Anne Marie, and finally the youngest boy Mark. We became very good friends and all five of us played together.

During the holidays, the menu was to my liking. The desserts were great. We had a gingerbread house and a *buche de Noel*, which is a pastry roll that represents a tree trunk with all its imperfections and leprechauns working on it. We also had *borche*, a beet consommé with sliced boiled egg and fresh cream. Meat was often a pork roast. I enjoyed all types of goodies that my mom and her lady cook made and friends brought over. Christmas in my mind was a time for food and gifts.

That Christmas, I wanted a bicycle. While I was still at school, my mother wrote a letter telling me that I would receive a bicycle, but it would not be new. My parents never tried to make me believe in Santa Claus. For me, it was normal that parents gave gifts to their children at Christmas time.

At last Christmas Eve came and my mom made all types of Polish food. We had a tradition during the meal when we split a very flat piece of unleavened bread that looked like a wafer that Catholics take during Holy Communion. Before we ate it, we wished each other good will.

The wafer was as big as a normal book page and as flat. In Polish it was called *opłatek*.

The holidays were cramped that year because the house was so small, but we had a tree. It smelled wonderful and had lots of tinsel. Some of the ornaments were made at home. I had made others in school. We also had candles on the tree. The candles were short and placed very carefully on the ends of the branches so the tree would not catch on fire. The candles were lit after our Christmas Eve dinner while everybody was watching. All the lights in the house were turned off and the tree looked magnificent. While the candles were burning, I lit sparklers and made all types of motions with my hands in the dark. I did not know why, but it felt good and serene.

However, there were no gifts for me yet. I could not wait to go to bed, because the tradition was that the gifts would appear the next morning. Without fail, the next morning I found my bicycle. As my mother had said, it was a used one, but I did not care. It looked great to me and I could not wait to ride it. A thought came to my mind: I hoped that Nono and Claudie received bicycles too.

That morning, Vigneux got bigger. I could go anywhere I wanted on my bicycle. Of course, I needed to check with my mother for permission first. But my village had no more secrets. I could rediscover the lake. I could ride my bike to the movies. André's world had just become a little bigger.

I was happy because Nono also received a bicycle and we could bike together. Now that we had what we wanted, we decided we needed something even better. Our bikes needed to be transformed into make-believe motorcycles. We needed noise. We were tired of making *brrrr, brrrr* noises with our mouths, so our ingenious minds came up with a great idea. Nono got some playing cards and we fastened them to the back wheels with clothes pins. Presto, we had our motorcycles.

Claudie did not get a bicycle, so I made sure that we spent time together. When I was with him, I had a different type of feeling. We did not do many physical games, except the luge on the stairs. Instead, we played games inside. We built things with a game called Mecano, which is made of all sorts of metal pieces that we used to build almost anything. Claudie and I built bridges, working cranes, wagons, and all types of toys that we could put wheels on.

After Christmas, the week before New Year's passed very quickly. I had ambiguous feelings about going back to school. However, I did not dare say anything because I knew that it would be futile. I remember very vividly one day when I was not playing. Instead, I was sitting on the front stairs of our house and reading *Selection*, the French *Reader's Digest*. There were two articles that kept my attention for a long time. One was about the United States, although I do not remember the content. The other one was called "The Most Unforgettable Character I Ever Met." Both articles changed my life to a certain degree. When I finished reading, I decided that I would live in America when I grew up. My other decision was to train myself to have control over everything I did. Yes, that second article was all about self-control.

So the holidays came and went. I had good times with my friends, but soon I would be on the train back to school. That day came quickly and after I got my suitcase ready, we were on our way to the train station. I noticed that I was much calmer than the first time. Experience must have done its job. Soon I would be with my school friends again and we would have a lot of stories to tell.

The train's whistle sounded. The doors closed with a clacking noise. I waved goodbye to my parents. School life was starting again.

Chapter 11

My decision to learn to be in control of myself made an enormous difference in my life. After Christmas vacation, I returned to school with very little trepidation. Soon, school experiences blended together with no distinct timelines. Before long, I was looking forward to another vacation. I was ready to rediscover Switzerland.

The Swiss people practice a tradition that goes back many years. Parents plan well in advance for their children to live with a family that speaks another language during school vacations. As a result, after the children have graduated and are young adults, they can speak the three main tongues. The children, who are away learning another language, are treated like members of the family. They have chores and other things that are demanded of all children. There is no difficulty organizing exchanges between families, because parents want to help their children learn.

I suppose I could count myself in that group. Even though my family was not from Switzerland, we had many friends in that country. Like any other child in the group, I spent time away from my family leaning French and German. Switzerland is a very small country and yet people have a choice of speaking four different tongues: French, German, Italian, or the true Suisse language called *Romanche*. To tell you the truth, *Romanche* is hardly ever spoken. The country is so small that four Switzerlands could fit into the state of Texas. Two could fill an area the size of France. I always enjoyed the brain-challenging idea of being able to speak the different tongues.

One winter, I spent time with some other children in a house that looked like a big chalet. Snow was everywhere and the chalet seemed to be standing alone among the white hills. I do not recall seeing another house or chalet close. I know it was not a school, since we did not have any classes. The chalet must have been a pension because all of us slept there. We had our meals together and we could never eat fast enough to go skiing. I remember very well that I had a lot of fun with the other children. Our main focus was to ski every day from morning to night

In the morning after breakfast, we dashed to the room where our skis were kept. From there, we went outside to see what kind of snow was on the ground. That was very important, because depending on the snow conditions, we waxed our skis with different waxes. Whether the snow was wet, dry, powdery, or somewhere in between, we chose the appropriate wax. It took some time to do it well because at that time the skis were made of wood, not man-made materials as they are now. To wax the skis, we put them upside down, supported on each end by a wooden horse. Then we dipped a cloth into the hard wax and just like waxing a car, we rubbed and rubbed until we could almost see ourselves reflected in the surface. Then, hurray, the day was ours.

We did not have anyone to supervise us. I suppose that the people who were responsible for us knew that we were also responsible. We did not have any ski lifts or special tracks, so we cross-country skied anywhere we wanted to. We did not have any special plans about where to go or what to do. We just wanted to ski. From time to time, when we found a good slope, we stopped and went up and down that slope until we got tired.

We knew we had to be back for lunch and we were. The lunch never went quickly enough. We wanted to go outside again as fast as we could. However, first we had to wax our skis again because the snow conditions had changed during the morning. Sometimes it snowed while we were skiing, so we needed another type of wax.

We came back to the chalet in the afternoon for the traditional *quatre heures*. At that time we had a bowl of coffee and bread with jam. To this day, I remember how good it felt to hold the hot bowl of coffee in my cold hands. The bread was big, round, and hot, and the crust was crispy. To cut it, we needed to hold it sideways against our chests and then carve a slice. Then we added butter and strawberry jam. It was better than good: it was delicious.

Afterwards, we stayed close to the chalet and instead of skiing, we luged. For the first time, I became acquainted with a luge that could actually be steered. Normally, we directed the luge by switching our weight from one side to the other. This luge had a wooden stick across the front that could be turned to the right or left. Everyone wanted to sit in front to be able to steer. We had great fun with the luge. Then we fell into the snow and started snowball fights. I do not remember ever quarreling with any of the other kids. We had a common goal and that was to have fun.

One memorable day, I decided in my grand wisdom to ski without ski poles. It was a great idea, I thought. So I went without poles for the day. I was the only one with no poles, but no one told me that maybe this was not a good idea. I felt great. We skied to a glacier and I remember skiing on ice with the other kids. Then we took off our skis and put on our shoes with some special picks so we could walk safely. We went back for lunch and the *quatre heures*, then continued our fun in the snow. That night we came back to the chalet, had dinner, and went to bed. The next morning I wanted to get up but I could not. My legs hurt so much that I could barely stand on them. Needless to say, for few days I was unable to walk, ski, luge, or even go up or down the stairs. Since then, I never skied without having the poles with me.

Now when I go to a restaurant that has displays of artifacts, I some-times find similar skis and luges from that time in Switzerland. It brings back fond memories and I just stand there staring until that certain feeling passes away.

When I was a teenager, I visited some of my father's friends during vacations. They were farmers and while I was there, I helped them in their daily farm routine. I enjoyed it and at the same time I learned a lot about animals and what it takes to bring food to the table. I also learned later from some letters that I found after my dad's death that for me it was a way to learn work discipline.

There are two trips that especially come to my mind. Both were part of my summer vacations. Usually I went to Switzerland by train. The train left Paris from the Gare de Lyon and traveled to Neuchatel, a town on the shore of Lake Neuchatel, or to Geneva, which is on the shore of Lake Geneva.

One particular trip was to visit the Gerardet family. I don't remember the particular village, but their farm was situated on top of a hill. There was a long, winding dirt road to get to their house. The farm was very compact. The big house was the first building that came into view. On the right was the horse barn. In the middle were more barns used mainly for storing some machines and hay. On the left was a large barn with about forty cows. In the middle of all those buildings, the ground was made of cobblestones. On the left of the big house was a big hill where vines grew. The big house had also a garage. The Gerardets owned a black car, called a standard, but I don't remember the make of this automobile. I do recall the entire farm as a very nice setting, as well as a busy one.

On this trip, my parents came with me. After one day they went back to Vigneux. I quickly settled in and was an integral part of the work force. I enjoyed it and although I could quit anytime I wanted, the idea of quitting never entered my mind. One of the first duties I chose was to help the *vacher*. *Vacher* is the French term for the person who takes care of the cows, including milking them. When I learned how to milk the cows, I had a round, one-legged stool that I fastened to my waist. I talked to the cow to let her feel that someone was behind her. Then I affixed her tail to one of her hind legs so it would not hit me in the eye. One time I did not take care of the cow's tail and, of course, I got hit. When I finished with one cow, I went on to the next one. I got up at four in the morning to milk the cows. We had to hurry because a truck came early and we had to load the large milk cans onto it. After that was done, we cleaned the stalls, which meant taking out the manure with a wheelbarrow and replacing it with clean straw.

I asked my parents to send me some rubber boots so I could do the job better. After I received the boots, I felt like a grown-up. The boots made me feel tall and strong. For the first time, I learned to use a pitchfork. I was very proud of myself. With the boots and the knowledge of how to use a pitchfork, I felt that I belonged to the farm work force and that I was doing my part.

There were two other workers, Antonio and Renateau. After a while, instead of milking the cows, I hitched one or two horses to a wagon. The mowing machine was attached behind the wagon. When I arrived at the destination, I hitched the horses to the mowing machine and mowed grass. After the mowing was done, I raked it and loaded it onto the wagon. Then I went back to the barn to feed the cows.

I loved to work on the farm. The mornings were beautiful and I loved the horses. I also helped spray manure on the fields. I sat on a wagon pulled by two horses. Then I went slowly back and forth across the field spraying. I liked doing this since it was easy and I was in control of the horses. This particular operation lasted almost the whole day. When I had more experience, I was sometimes permitted to drive a tractor under supervision.

I also worked in the garden. I harvested currants, blackberries, and raspberries. I helped in the kitchen too, but I liked working outside best.

One of the jobs that I did not particularly like was working in the vineyard. It was tedious work and the vineyard was so large that it seemed that the work would never be finished.

I enjoyed harvesting hay. Four of us did this job. We mowed the hay and let it dry. It took several days before we could harvest it. Then I helped hitch the horses to two wagons and we loaded them with hay. Sometimes I was the person on the wagon receiving the hay and piling it in such a way that it would not fall. Since we did this in summer, loading the hay was a very hot experience.

The best time I had was when I helped in the stable. I had a very good relationship with the horses. They never kicked me or even tried. By talking to the horses when I was coming behind them, I avoided surprises since they knew that I was there. I fed them and cleaned their stalls, took the manure out, and replaced it with fresh, clean straw.

When I took care of the horses, my job was to stand in front of the animals and, when prompted, to move them forward. I took the horses by their bits and moved them ahead. One day while I was doing this, it was very hot and the horse flies were big and nasty. The horses were agitated and when I took them to move forward, one bit me on the right shoulder. I got very upset and I punched the horse's nose. It seemed to settle the horses down and I did not have any more problems. Another day when it was very hot and everyone was tired, the owner took the three of us to a café before we went back to the farm. It was for me a wonderful moment, because I felt I was part of the men.

While with the Gerardet family, I experienced one disaster and one near-disaster. The big barn behind the main house was used for storing hay for the year and for storing the farm machines. One day two young girls about the same age as I were playing with sparklers. It was during the daytime and they decided to go into the barn so the sparklers would shine in the dark. I saw them go there and even asked why they were going, but I didn't think about possible consequences. After a short time, while I was hitching a horse to wagon, I noticed smoke coming out from the barn. Both girls ran away and I started to yell "Fire! Fire!" The barn went up in flames, but the farm workers and Mr. Gerardet saved a few of the farm machines. The police and the firemen came, but only the other buildings could be protected.

I felt very important because I was the first one who called for help. The police wanted all types of information about what had happened. For the rest of the afternoon, I was an important person. When I told my parents what had happened, my dad wanted to know if the police had been nice to me. I did not understand the whole ramifications of what that fire meant. The only thing I knew was that I was important for a time.

The near-disaster was my own doing. I loved that black car and when the occasion presented itself, I went close to it. When I could, I opened the door and put my head inside. One day, the occasion was at last there. No one was around and the car was unlocked. I opened the door and I found the keys in the ignition. I sat in the driver's seat and pretended that I was going somewhere, although I didn't know where. I was so excited to be inside. I looked at all the gauges and they were shiny and impressive to me. The stick shift had a wooden knob at its end. I did not know that one of the gears was engaged. When I turned the key and pushed the starter button, the car moved forward, but the engine did not start. I got very scared and left the car precipitously, not even closing the door. For a while, I did not look for any more excitement than I could handle.

My stay with the Gerardet family was not all work. The whole experience of being with them was fantastic. We visited their family and I loved to be in that black car. It felt good. The inside was made of leather and it smelled wonderful. One weekend, the family went to a town called Nyon, situated on the shores of Lake Geneva. A helicopter took people for rides over the town of Nyon. The price was twenty Suisse cents for two people. I was permitted to fly with another person. It was my very first time in a helicopter and I was scared, but I never let anyone know. I was fascinated by the big boats on Lake Geneva. They were from France and Italy and it was exciting to me that there were different nationalities in such a small area.

I had another passion, cycling. The Tour de France, the professional bicycle race, took place in July. The competitors were from many countries and for me that time was very important. I wrote to my parents so they would send me *l'Equipe*, a sports newspaper that gave all types of daily information about the race. Just before the Tour de France, the Tour de Suisse started and I went with the Gerardet family to see the race pass by. For me, at the time it was the ultimate excitement.

Finally, it was time for me to go back home to my parents in France. School was again in the horizon. But my thoughts were already starting to focus on more Suisse summers.

Chapter 12

My summer vacations lasted about three months. I spent time with my parents at the beginning. Then, for most of the summer, I lived with families in other countries. I often went to Switzerland where my dad had two very good friends. Before school started again, I returned to my parents for a few weeks.

When I compare my life at that time to life in the United States, or even in some parts of Europe, I realize that I did not have what others might consider a family life. Instead, I had family experiences. Now that I am older and looking at my own children and grandchildren, my philosophy has changed from knowing to wondering. Both ways are good. However, it's very difficult to choose which lifestyle would be best for a certain family. When I was a child I was determined to make the best of every situation.

One Suisse summer, I lived with my father's friends, the Gentizons, who lived across Neuchatel Lake in Lugnore, a small village with a small paved road. The Gentizons were farmers, but they did not have any animals. Instead, they grew wheat, colza, potatoes, green beans, and many other products. They had a lot of machines that could harvest almost anything. Actually, they were set up so well with farm machines that other farmers from villages around Lugnore used the Gentizons as contractors for harvesting their own fields.

The Gentizons had two sons, Gaston and Daniel, who were older than I. Later during my stay, Gaston had to serve in the Suisse military school. His departure made it difficult for the family because it was during the harvest. In Switzerland, all the males serve four months at a time.

I do not remember for how many years, but I think it was for about ten years. Since Gaston was away, the family was happy to have me to help. It made me feel very good to be needed. There were many tasks that I liked to do and, of course, some that I did not like at all. However, they all had to be done.

Besides the two boys, the Gentizon family included Mr. Gentizon, his wife, and their daughter Francine. She was a great help at harvest time during her three-week vacation. Suisse vacations were related to agriculture so children could help with the planting, harvesting, and other activities. I do not remember Francine's age, but at the farm, age did not mean a great deal. As long as a person could walk, a task was given.

There were two particular situations that I disliked while I stayed at the house. The Gentizons were Protestant and religious. Their idea of what was right sometimes did not agree with my young man's beliefs. For example, I liked jazz very much. On Sundays after a religious gathering, we came home and I searched for a jazz station on the radio. After a while, I knew where to find the station, but I had to be very careful while I listened. The sound had to be so low that my ear touched the radio. Still, whenever I was discovered listening to jazz, I was told to turn off the radio because it was "savage music." Obviously, I was not very happy and it was a struggle every Sunday between the Gentizons and me.

The second unhappy situation was at night. I slept in the formal dining room on a sofa bed. Besides my sleeping arrangement, the room had a table with a lace tablecloth, a matching credenza, and, on the opposite wall a clock that chimed every fifteen minutes. For some reason, the family did not want to stop the tick-tock and chiming of that infamous clock. After several nights of not sleeping very well, I decided to take matters into my own hands. Every night at about ten o'clock when everyone was in bed, I managed to open the glass and I stopped the pendulum with my fingers. In the morning I started the pendulum and moved the clock's hands to the correct time.

Everyone got up at four o'clock and after a quick morning clean-up, all the members of the family harvested strawberries before breakfast. The large strawberry field was close to the house. Each member took a row and picked strawberries, putting them in shallow wooden crates. In the beginning, I ate as much as I could. Of course, I also had to make sure that my crate got full. We harvested the berries until about seven. Then we stacked all the crates on top of one another by the dirt road where a truck came to pick them up. The strawberry harvest went straight to the market.

The women left the field to start breakfast while the crates were being stacked. The breakfast was good, except for the ham. The menu had coffee, bread, pan-fried potatoes, and ham. I complained to my parents that the ham had too much fat. Was I ahead of my time? However, breakfast was a very good time for me. It provided rest, most of the food was to my liking, and I had fun participating in the family conversations.

After the meal, we went to another task in the field. There were many tasks, depending of the weather. One task I did not care for was harvesting potatoes. Daniel was responsible for digging the potatoes from the ground, but he did not do it by hand. Instead, he used a machine that looked like a cannon with a big wheel on the end of the barrel. That machine was pulled by a tractor and the big wheel turned and dug the potatoes out of the ground. Behind the machine were four or six people with baskets. It took four people per row to harvest the potatoes. The first two picked the bigger ones, which went to the market. The next two people took the small ones that were used for food for the pigs. It was a task that usually lasted most of the day if it was not raining. The women worked until it was time for them to prepare the meals.

Around ten o'clock, everyone stopped working for about half an hour. For me, it was a perfect time, not only because I did not have to pick up potatoes then, but also because the food the women brought was delicious. We had fresh, hot, crispy bread that was delivered every day by car. The bread was round and when I cut it, I could see the steam flowing from it. With the bread we had cheese, jam, and cider.

Let me describe this cider. It was a delight for the mouth and the taste buds. The family made the cider from their apples and put it in small wooden barrels stored in a basement under the main house. The basement was more like a small cave with black dirt for the walls and the floor, so the temperature was constant in summer or winter. After a period of time, the apple juice fermented and had natural bubbles when served. It was not refrigerated, but cold enough from being stored in the cave. I don't know how long it took to make the cider, but it was the most wonderful cider I've ever had. To this day, whenever I think about it, my mouth waters.

Alas, any good time has to come to an end. After we finished eating, harvesting potatoes was again on the agenda. We had to put the potatoes in sacks and load them onto a cart to take them to the farm house where a truck picked them up. The women left the field at dusk to prepare supper, which was eaten in the kitchen. The room was very large and had a thick wooden table and heavy benches on either side. Before supper we washed, which took a long time. Dried mud was hard to get rid of. We also had to change our shoes and pants before we were ready to come into the kitchen.

The next morning was a repeat: strawberries, breakfast, and then Mr. Gentizon's deciding the task or tasks for that day. If it was raining, my luck diminished. During rainy days, we could not do field work. However, in one of the barns were several carts with onions that needed to be taken care of. Everyone, except the women, was expected to work on the onions. The work consisted of taking each onion and removing the first two layers of skin so that a nice clean yellow skin was left. After we did that, we put the onions into deep, wooden crates. By the end of the day, we had to have enough crates filled for the truck to come to pick them up. Needless to say, we all smelled like onions. However, that was not the problem. After the whole day peeling those onions, there was nothing that anyone could do to get rid of the smell. So for several days after a rain, all the men smelled like onions and we were made aware of that by the women. Of course, it was all in fun.

The best time and task for me was when the wheat and colza harvests were ready. The colza seed was used to make cooking oil. Most of the other farmers came to the Gentizon's to help us work twenty-four hours per day, so we had three teams of two people each working eight hours per day. It was fun for me for few reasons. First, I liked to feel needed. It made me feel important; it felt that I was doing something that only I could do. Also, I liked machines and mostly I wanted to drive.

During one harvest time I was introduced to the Ford Ferguson tractor. I drove the tractor to the field where the harvester was attached to it. For me, both machines were exciting. The tractor was open and had bars to rest my feet on each side. I had to shuffle my feet between the clutch and those bars. The accelerator on the right side of the steering wheel was manned by hand. The exciting time was when the tractor was moving, since there was no floor and I could see the ground passing under the tractor. I loved to feel the power under me. The tractor had front and back hydraulics that were used for different machines.

The harvester was my responsibility. It was a tall machine with a metallic ladder that I used to get to the top. The top of the machine was flat with the big wheel that directed the wheat to be cut on the right side.

On top, the harvester had four openings and I had to affix burlap bags to each opening. On the top right side behind the big wheel, but much higher, was a slide through which I had to eject the bags full of grain to the ground. The bags were picked up later by a cart pulled by another tractor. I was good at what I was doing. However, one time I suppose I did not focus enough. After I readied a bag to be ejected, I pulled the lever to open the shoot and the bag caught my foot. Both of us ended on the ground. I did not get hurt, but it was embarrassing. For a time, I was the main character in a funny story.

Sometimes I worked during the night. I enjoyed working under the lights from the harvester and tractor. One benefit of working at night was that we ate a lot of rabbits. When the rabbits saw the lights, they stayed stationary and the combine did the rest. I know that in the United States, rabbit might not be a culinary delicacy, but in the old country it is a very common dish.

There was something special about working during the night. The sky was dark and full of stars. Even though there was noise from the tractor and the harvester, I felt as though I were encircled by silence and a feeling of well-being. The lights of the tractor and combine did not disturb the peaceful feeling. After a while, we stopped and had bread with Swiss cheese and cider that I liked so much. The bread and cheese somehow tasted so much better during those nights.

I think that during those harvest times, I learned to appreciate nature. The smell of the cut wheat in the coolness of the night and the sky full of stars are things I will never forget. When it was time for us to go home to rest, I was already thinking about going back and doing it again. At that time, it did not feel like work to me. Instead, it was a new experience, a kind of freedom that I was not in control of, but it felt good and I did not want to do anything to change that.

Harvesting lasted about three weeks. After we finished cutting the wheat and colza, we had to gather the straw and bring it to the barn. To collect the straw, we used another machine which was also pulled by tractor. The machine amassed the straw into a square, then tied it with a string. Using pitchforks, two of us loaded each square onto a cart. It was hard work, but I enjoyed it. When the harvest finished, everything became normal again. No more rushing, no more night work. It felt like a page had turned over and a new chapter was starting.

Not far from Lugnore was another village called Montmagny. I could go from one village to another by bicycle. In Montmagny was a small pension house that belonged to another Gentizon family member. After the harvest, my mother came to visit and both of us stayed there. The pension was a two-story house with a big kitchen and a huge table. The formal dining room had a table covered with a lace tablecloth. However, that table was much smaller compared to the one in kitchen. All the furniture in the kitchen was made of rustic wood.

On the second floor were a few rooms. The room where my mother and I stayed faced a dirt road going to the center of the village. In the room were two iron beds, a sink, and a big porcelain pitcher for water so we could wash our faces and hands.

In front of the house the ground was covered with cobblestones. On the left was a fence that separated the house from a large orchard. Around the fence were blackberry, boysenberry, and raspberry bushes. Gooseberry bushes grew further towards the orchard. Just across from the house was a small barn where small animals, hay, and small machines were all together. Rabbits, chickens, two pigs, and two cows lived in the barn. One of the small machines was very interesting. It had only two wheels in front. On top of the wheels was a small engine. On the back was a very small platform where a worker could stand. Extending from the wheels were two big handles like those on a motorcycle. From there, a person steered and controlled the speed. That small motorized machine could pull a regular-size, loaded cart.

On the cobblestones in front of the house was a wooden chair that could not be moved. That chair was reserved for the house master and no one else could sit in it. He was the oldest Gentizon alive. He always wore a *casquette*, a flat hat with a visor that looked like a cap. He had a long, salt-and-pepper beard. The old man was stooped over and walked with a cane. He always had good things to say to everyone. He enjoyed having people sit around him because then he could do what he loved most: tell stories.

When I was in Montmagny, life was easy. No more physical hard work, even though I would help on many occasions. The orchard was one of my favorite places because it had two types of trees: cherry and apple. At the time, it was cherry season and I, along with another worker, harvested the cherries for the market. Every morning, I hung a deep, circular basket on the side of my pants and filled it up. However, I loved cherries and before I filled the basket, I ate my fill. I learned one very important lesson while harvesting cherries. To be able to stay on a ladder for a long period, I needed shoes with thick soles. Otherwise, after a short time my feet ached and I had to get down. The orchard had two types of cherry trees. One cherry was completely dark red and the other one was half yellow and half light red. The second type was slightly bigger. Both were very tasty, but to me, as long as they were cherries, I ate them.

In the afternoon, we enjoyed leisure time. I loved to go to the orchard to sit under the shady side of a tree and just relax. I either fell asleep or just looked at nature's paradise. I had only to extend my hand to get almost any fruit available. It was quiet and peaceful. Far away, I could hear cow bells, a light breeze in the trees, and an occasional farmer on a Vespa scooter passing by on the dirt road, probably headed for the village.

When five o'clock in the afternoon came, the whole atmosphere changed. I called it pig time. Around Montmagny were other very small farms which also had pigs. Little did I know that pigs have embedded clocks. Every day at five o'clock, the pigs started to squeal. Their noise could be heard from miles away. People often checked their watches to assure themselves the watches were correct. Even the two pigs in the small barn joined the cacophony. Their noise was also a sign for everyone to start doing things. At the pension the kitchen started bustling. I helped prepare green beans for cooking. I also ground the coffee. After I added the coffee beans to the grinder, I sat on a chair, put the grinder between my legs, and turned the handle. I did not like to do that because I wore shorts and the grinder pinched my thighs every time it got stuck.

At the pension, I did not care for any animals. Whatever work I did was on a voluntary basis. It was fun since I was in control. In the morning after the two cows were milked, I went with one of the workers to deliver the milk to the cheese house located on the main road in Montmagny. I was interested in the whole process. Our milk was filtered, then emptied into a huge vat where it was moved around and around by very big paddles. Eventually, the milk turned into cheese.

Some of my best times at the pension were spent learning to play the accordion. Two other young people from the village came to visit me to play the accordion. I suppose I had a gift for music, because by the time I departed from Switzerland, I could play easily. However, playing this instrument put me into a direct confrontation with my parents, not in Switzerland, but later on when I was at home. I wanted to play the accordion, but my parents wanted me to continue playing the piano. We went back and forth and I decided that if I could not play the accordion,

I would not play the piano. I even went further and decided that I would not speak Polish anymore. Of course, I regretted my decisions later on.

I enjoyed being with my mother at the pension. One Sunday we visited the medieval town of Mora. To get there, we had to cross Lake Mora on the ferry. It was a beautiful town where cars were not allowed. Tourists walked up the cobble-stoned road bordered by side-walk cafés. The wall surrounding the small village had been used to protect it against attacks. My mother and I walked on the wall and I tried to imagine how the long-ago defenders must have felt.

During the days at the pension, we enjoyed doing our own things. At supper everyone came together and the food was great. The best for me was the dessert. The lady of the house, whom I called *Tantinette*, made apple tarts that were out of this world. Sometimes at the table I was singled out to help peel the apples. When the weather was nice, we ate outside. A table was set on the cobblestones and the master of the house said a prayer before the food was served. The supper was a long affair. No one was in a hurry and everybody was included in the conversation. It reminded me of pictures of Italian weddings with everybody around the table.

After the meal, my mom and I often went for walks. If it was late, we just went to bed. One morning when I woke up, my mother asked if I had felt my bed moving. I did not know why she asked that question until she told me that during that night there was a small earthquake. I did not believe her until she showed me that my bed had moved from one side of the room to the middle.

In Montmagny I had a close encounter with fireworks. During the national holiday, a group of us went to the plaza to see the festivities. Afterwards, everybody lit firecrackers. I had some, but I don't know what kind. I was told to put the wooden tail end into a bottle and to light the other end. When I did that, the firecracker went towards the sky with a swooshing sound. After a very short time, it exploded and its lights fell toward the ground. As soon as the firecracker left the bottle, I put my fingers in my ears because the noise disturbed me. Once again, I was having flashbacks to the bombings.

People didn't know about Post Traumatic Stress Disorder when I was a child. Doctors gave me syrups and my parents did their best to help me. In 1980, when PSTD was finally given a name, I realized I'd been through all that. I think that PTSD has a place, but at the same time, I think some people take advantage of it. All along, I wanted to take responsibility for myself. I decided as a child that I didn't want to give in, so I was determined to overcome my symptoms. Much later, I discovered a letter that my mother wrote to my father when she and I were in Spain. I was 15 or 16 at that time and she told him that I was doing well. Suddenly, I realized that it had been a therapeutic trip, like the Suisse summers my parents planned for me.

Eventually, summer came to an end. My mother and I got a ride to Cudrefin, a boat-landing on Lake Neuchatel. We took the boat across the lake to the train station and, after sleeping on the train, we arrived in Paris. School was around the corner. I was a little concerned because I knew I was going to a different boarding school. However, there was a bright side to the change: my best friend Dodo, who went to École des Roches with me, was also going to the new school.

Chapter 13

École St. Augustin was an international school with students from many countries and branches in several parts of France and in Canada. Since the school was not far from where I lived, it was the first time that my parents did not have to travel a long way to visit me. I even could go home on weekends if my grades were satisfactory. The school also had a program called *semi-pension* for students who lived close by. They came for the day and went home at night.

In comparison to the other schools I attended, École St. Augustin was a small school, although it had several centers. First was the educational center where all the classes were situated. The buildings were in a line all on one side. The courtyard where we had our recess was in front. In the middle of the yard there were trees in a line that split the recess court. The whole complex was encircled by a high wall.

The second center was the sports complex. During my school days, sports complexes were not very fancy. We had a soccer field with a cinder track around it. On one side was a sand pit for high and long jump competitions. The locker room was an old wooden shack.

Valparaiso, the third center, was in another part of town, about one mile from the classrooms. This is where all students ate and slept. The complex of several buildings had a big garden atmosphere. There were trees, flowers, and shrubs of all kinds. The whole center was very comfortable.

My second-floor dormitory had a staircase leading to our rooms. At the top, a hallway stretched from a large landing. The rooms branched out from this hallway. Five students slept in my room. I was lucky because my best friend Dodo was in the same room as I. The third boy, whom I will call K, was a student from Russia. Another, whose name I've forgotten, was the son of the owner of the biggest trucking company in France. I do not remember anything about the fifth boy.

As in the previous boarding schools, we each had a place for our clothes and care packages. Instead of pillows, we had very hard bolsters. Later in the year, we had some fun with bolster fights when no one was looking. The first night was lonely. However, having my best friend with me felt good.

Since this was not my first experience in boarding school, I was used to the discipline and regulations. Also, by then I was older and maybe smarter, so I tried not to put myself in precarious situations. My plan was not always successful.

The first day was like every day. The bonus was that I did not have to go to Mass in the mornings. We all had to get ready for breakfast at seven, but the food was nothing to brag about. There were two refectory rooms separated in the middle by a much smaller room where the professors ate. I do not recall the names of all my professors, but I do remember many of their personalities and their nicknames. Large wooden tables were lined up against both walls and in two rows in the middle. The seating was provided on long wooden benches, which accommodated six students each. There was one bench on each side of the table. We were not told with whom to sit. However, after we made our choice, we were not able to change.

The menu was not fancy at all. We had *café au lait* and pieces of bread. We also had different flavors of jam, but not all at the same time. Each day another flavor was served. Breakfast was served by four women who worked in the kitchen. They had a big rolling table with coffee pots and a big basket full of bread. The coffee was served in a big bowl, which we held with both hands to be able to drink from it. Boys sitting by the wall had to be good catchers because the women threw the bread underhanded to them. We got one piece at a time, but the women went around and handed out bread until we all had our fill. When breakfast was over, we made a line, two-by-two, and walked through the streets to our classes.

Lunch was not much better. The food was mostly noodles with cheese and bread. Meat was seldom on the menu. The meals were served in the old military style. The women pushed huge wheeled pots, usually filled with noodles, and slapped the food onto the plates we were holding.

We called that dish "swimming noodles." We liked Thursday's menu of blood sausage, called *boudin*, and real French fries. The problem was that I only had one piece of *boudin* and seven French fries. I complained to the professor in charge and to my surprise he took our side. It was a decision that all the students enjoyed. When dessert, which was mostly jam, was served, we could talk and go to our care packages to supplement our sweet tooth.

While we ate, the professor we nicknamed Rhino read us stories. Since we could not talk during meals, the stories were welcomed. However, there was a twist. Sometimes if the professor was unsure that we were listening, he directed us to write a summary for the next day. If a student did not provide his work the next day, his free weekend evaporated.

The discipline was like in any other boarding school I had attended. However, at École St. Augustin we had to meet ten specific criteria with ten points each before our parents could come to visit or we could go home for the weekend. The school's dean, who lived on the grounds, visited all classes every day. In the mornings, he made sure that the classes were in good order. We knew that he would come on a daily basis, but it was never at the same time. On Saturdays, we were not dismissed until he came and looked at our booklets for the total points from our criteria. We needed a minimum of fifty points to be able to visit with parents or go home for the two days. If we had a zero in any criterion, we would be grounded for the weekend.

Because of the international nature of École St. Augustin, foreign languages were emphasized. Everybody had to study two foreign languages, English and Spanish, plus a third one of the student's choice. Obviously, we had to choose from a prepared list. I was lucky because I spoke Polish at home, so I did not have to choose a third one. However, Latin was for everyone because French has its roots in that language.

To enter the classroom, we had to make a double line and be quiet. After the teacher gave us the sign to go in, we had to stand until we had permission to sit. Some of the teachers had zero tolerance about poor behavior in class, while others were more lenient.

Our first English professor was very easy on us. We took advantage of him many, many times. However, I am not sure if that was because he let us or because he was not able to control his class as a result of his age. To us, he seemed to be an old man. He always wore a dark suit with a grey overcoat and a black hat from which his long, white hair flowed. He always had an umbrella with him, whether it rained or not. Even though we took advantage of him, we liked him and he was a good English professor. He was one of few who had a personality. He was not with the school the following year.

Most of our professors wore grey smocks with buttons in front to protect their clothes. Those smocks made them look all alike. Our French teacher, Mr. Gourlet, was a smock-wearing professor from a part of France called Brittany. People from that area are called Bretons and are considered to be very stubborn, which was proven in class time and time again. He was a good professor, fair, nothing exciting, just requiring hard work.

Mr. Levesque, who taught science and physics, was short and stocky and had a wart on the top of his nose. We nicknamed him Rhino, not to make fun of him, but to put him at our level since most of us had nicknames. He was always well dressed and very helpful to us. We knew that if we were in trouble, he would help. Mr. Levesque was the man who read to us during breakfast, lunch, and supper. I liked him very much because he was unpretentious, quiet, but always ready to support us.

Our new English teacher was Mr. Bruno. Even when we were talking among ourselves, no one ever called him just Bruno. There was something mysterious about that word "Mr." in relation to Professor Bruno. We were never able to figure him out. In class he was very sharp and demanding. The advantage we had with our first English professor was gone. Our feeling was preservation at all costs.

However, our English knowledge jumped ten-fold. In class we had to speak entirely in English. All questions had to be asked in English, even the written ones. Mr. Bruno was a big man with very large hands. When he pointed a finger towards any one of us, we had better have the right answer to whatever question he asked. His questions were not necessarily about the current moment in class; many times he demanded answers about past classes. Not knowing the answers was costly in terms of the weekend.

Yet, Mr. Bruno was very much liked. His personality was such that we felt comfortable when we needed support or help with anything. Sometimes he took our side and asked other professors to be more lenient with us. When we thought that he was very hard on us, he surprised us by behaving in a fatherly manner. However, for no reason at all, at least in our minds, he could be our worst nightmare.

Sometimes when we played soccer on the school grounds, the ball went over a wall to somebody else's property. One day Mr. Bruno let us go over the wall to fetch it. The next day with exactly the same situation, he admonished us just for asking to get the ball. But he was one of those professors whom the students liked for no apparent reason. As for myself, I have very warm memories of him and I am glad that I met him in my lifetime.

One teacher took the trophy for being the most *avant garde*, personable, and fun, as well as being a good professor. He was very tall. His hair and mustache were red. His daily attire showed his non-conformist attire. While the average staff member wore grey with a long smock, he came to his class with brilliant, red-orange pants and a yellow or light colored jacket with a white tee-shirt underneath. His shoes were any color but black.

In class, he walked from side to side in front of us on the small podium. He always kept his right hand in the back pocket of his pants and held a lit cigarette in his left hand. His mustache was discolored on one side from the nicotine. To teach, he never looked in a book. We wondered how he knew everything about economics and marketing by heart. While he was teaching, we took notes, but we had no books, no homework, and no weekly tests. It was a pleasure to learn from him because he made it so simple and interesting. We were not under any pressure from tests or from failing.

This professor owned a motorcycle which he rode from the educational campus to Valparaiso where we had our meals. His motorcycle made a lot of noise and we liked that. He was not afraid to open up his machine to full throttle for the ride to Valparaiso.

He was also my fencing teacher. He himself was a very accomplished fencer. We fenced in an old gymnasium where the light was provided by bulbs swinging from very long electric wires. A humorous moment happened one day when both of us were ready to fence. We saluted one another by elevating our foils to our faces. Then, because he was so tall, his foil hit one of the bulbs and it exploded. At first we did not know what had happened, but as soon as the bulb fell to the floor, we started laughing.

Our professor lived at the school, so we saw him every day, not only in class, but also during meals and at bedtime. He was not involved directly with our lives outside the classroom, but seeing him in the professors' dining room was always reassuring. A misfortune happened one day while he was walking from side to side on the small podium in our classroom. He took one too many steps, fell from the podium, and broke his ankle.

As with any situation, there is always someone who is remembered negatively. Such a person was Professor Martin. We called him "Mr." too, among ourselves, but no one really respected that title. He was very mischievous and always tried to find something wrong. His specialty was surprising students. I remember one of the surprises. Professor Martin liked to place himself inside doorways. When students passed in front of him, he clasped of his hands on both sides of the boy's face. He was so well-known for his antics that students, not knowing if they had done something wrong or not, ducked instantly when they passed by him.

Life at the school was good, but all schools have bullies. In our group there was a student who was obnoxious and who bothered everybody in our class. One day when it was raining, he and I had an argument. He was wearing a long, gray smock, probably to hide his obesity. While arguing, I pointed a finger at him. He got scared thinking that maybe I was going to hit him and he fell backwards into a puddle. I started to run away, knowing very well that he would get up and take care of me since he was much bigger. I was running and looking back at the same time, so I did not see the first tree and I hit it with my head. I lost to the tree by a knockout and found myself in the infirmary. I think that it was all for the best because the bully never bothered any one of us again.

I was involved in another conflict which had an influence on my future life. A Russian student said some nasty things about the Polish people, although he did not know that my family and I were Polish. One night during supper while we were eating soup, I emptied my soup bowl on his head. Of course, we started to fight and were separated by a few professors. I knew we were going to be punished, but I did not know when.

At nine o'clock I rushed upstairs to my room before anyone else and picked up a bolster from my bed. Then I went to his room and hid behind the door. It seemed as though I waited for a long time before he came to his room. As soon as he came through the door, I hit him over the head with the bolster. Even today I can see him clutching his neck, falling to the floor, and not moving. He stayed that way for some time and I felt an emptiness in my chest and a helpless feeling. My first thought was that I had killed him. At the moment he fell to the floor, I promised myself that I would never again fight or hit anyone. To this day, I have kept that promise.

Soon the professors came and in a way I was glad because they took over and I was not alone any more. The Russian boy ended up in the infirmary with dislocated vertebrae, but he was alive. I did not care about my punishment. The only thing that was important to me was that he was alive. Several of my weekends disappeared and I had to do extra school work.

This experience also changed my views about certain aspects of Catholicism. That night, as part of my punishment, I had to kneel in the hallway and say my prayers aloud. While I recited the prayers that somebody else had written, I realized I was also having several conversations in my head. I was thinking about spending a weekend with a girlfriend, playing an upcoming soccer game... all sorts of different things.

Suddenly I thought to myself that this was not religion as I wanted it to be. In school, I had been taught about many world religions. At home, since my mother was Catholic and my father was Jewish, we often had discussions about religion. The more I thought about prayer, the more I decided that religion needed only one word, trust. I decided to create my own prayers, so I would have to concentrate on what I was thinking and saying. This was a significant step in a lifetime of exploration of my religious beliefs.

Sports were also important to me during my stay at École St. Augustin. I had the opportunity to learn *pelot*, a Spanish game which uses a small ball a little bigger than a golf ball. Players use their bare hands to strike the ball against a *fronton*, a flat wall. Almost everybody played *pelot* during recess between classes.

The most popular game was football, which is soccer in the United States. We had only two teams of six players each, Poirrier and André. Poirrier was a French student one year older than I; he was a very good pupil and an outstanding soccer player. Everybody wanted to be on his team. He had already been chosen by a professional second division team in Paris called Red Star.

André's team was also good. When I was in school, a first division professional team talked to my parents and me about my abilities. At every recess, we chose five other teammates and started to play until we were called to class. For a soccer ball, we used a tennis ball. It was a competitive encounter, but also very friendly. We did not need any referees and there were no arguments. Both teams were more interested in developing a style of play and practicing it.

Besides soccer, we had sports every day at our sports complex, which was nothing to brag about. We practiced track and field most of the time. I was good at running. However, a lad called Gontier was the best runner of all. I tried to beat him many times and never achieved it. He also was a good friend of mine outside of school.

One day when we were competing against other schools, I was entered in the high and long jumps. Little did I know that this day would be a thorn in my side --- or, more correctly, my back, for many years. After jumping, we fell into the sand pit which had a cement border so the sand would not scatter. When I took my first high jump, my foot hit the cement border and that stopped me from falling naturally. I felt a twinge in my back, but did not give it any more thought. When I landed in the sand after my long jump, the pain was intolerable and I stood there unable to move. For the next twenty-plus years, I had back problems.

On Saturdays after the dean made his rounds, we watched movies in the gymnasium. My best friend Dodo and I sat together to see a story about the life of a merchant marine. I do not remember the story, but Dodo and I were so impressed that we promised each other that this is what we wanted to do. We decided that on our next trip home, we would approach our parents and sell them the idea. When the time came, we made our pitch, but I have to say that we were not surprised when our decision sank like a ton of bricks. A few weeks later, we forgot all about our brilliant idea.

I had another friend whose last name was Brest. He had lost his father, and his mother was unable to control him, so Dodo and I adopted him. We made him part of our school life and I made him part of my life outside of school too. When his mother came to school, she was very grateful that he had two friends. He was a good person and a good student when he was with us. At the end of school when everyone went his own way, Brest somehow disappeared. I thought I knew where I could find him, but it was to no avail. A few years later when I made my first trip to France from my new country, the United States, I went to visit his mother. Alas, she did not know where he was either and I never heard from him again.

Finally, my last school year at École St. Augustin came to an end. Along with the other students, I went to another learning institution for two days of testing. The first day's written tests and the second day's oral tests covered a variety of subjects that we had studied throughout our schooling. When the results were published in July, we went back to our schools to see if our names were on the list. Anyone whose name was not on the list had to redo the year. Luckily, I found my name and I received my Bachelor's in Business Administration.

My next step was the Sorbonne in Paris for my Master's in Marketing. My life was changing from that of a young student to a more adult life. Even though I still had my parents to guide me, I felt that I had to take responsibility for myself. That idea put me at odds with my parents many times, but I kept trying to fly from the nest.

Chapter 14

My life in Vigneux did not feel like a string of days coming in and going by. Instead, it was very much like a jigsaw puzzle. From the time I arrived in France, I felt like a salesman stopping to change clothes before continuing to the next destination. These memories may not be in chronological order, but they comprise a series of new beginnings in my life.

These new beginnings were a mixture of good and bad. I mostly felt in control of the bad because I was the one making the decisions to hurt my parents when I did not get my way. Controlling more Post Traumatic Stress Disorder symptoms was a real struggle. The good always seemed to happen regardless of what I did or did not do.

After we had lived for a long time in the small, shack-like house, my parents decided to build a new house on the same property. While I was away in different schools, my mother spent months designing our new home. For me it was exciting, since it was the first time that we were going to have a house like other people. I could not believe how talented my mother was. She not only designed the house, but she also designed the landscaping so precisely that all the flowers had places. She spent many hours with the architect to make sure she would get what she wanted.

Every time I came home from school, I was excited to see the progress. But I had to pay a price for all this. The tree where I had dreamed of riding all over the world had to go. The oval lawn where I played soccer with my tutor was moved and used for other purposes. Even the jungle disappeared as my mother organized everything. I thought about it and decided those things were all part of my past. Our home was the new beginning.

When it was finished, our new ranch house was beautiful. It had a basement and a garage under the house. A marble terrace circled half-way around the house. To get to the heavy, wooden doors, there were five marble stairs that occupied half of the front of the house. When inside, we could descend to the basement and garage or we could climb five more marble stairs to a large, marble area that opened to the various rooms. There, my parents received friends, took their coats, and showed them to the salon or the dining room.

I had my very own room with a glass door that reached all the way from the floor to the ceiling and overlooked the marble terrace and the flower garden. It was something to see and I loved to come home from school. At night during the summer, I slept with the big doors open so I could see the black sky illuminated by the moon. I played a game with my mind, and after a while, I became addicted to the exercise. The goal was to think about everything I knew about space. When I had all the planets and stars, including the moon and the sun, well-defined in my mind, I began to eliminate them one by one. The process was slow because I had to focus on each item before deleting it. At the end of the exercise, only the black emptiness was left and I deleted that too. But when I reached that point, I could not think any further and this is what was so addictive. I wanted to be able to think further, but I never could.

My war experiences, even though I was very young at the time, had left me with a lot of challenges, some bad, some good, and some bizarre. While I was going back and forth between my schools and home, another effect of the PTSD started. For no apparent reason, I could no longer talk in a normal fashion. I began to stutter and that became very annoying. Not only was I shy, but now I had to find a way to express myself without sounding foolish. Needless to say, my social life went south. In school I was often ridiculed. The biggest problem was that during my education we had oral exams and stuttering made passing them difficult.

I do not remember what my parents did about it, but as far as I know, I did not see any doctors, so I decided to help myself. I tried everything: breathing correctly, starting my sentences with a consonant, making ges-tures with my arms …. Anything I could think of, I tried. But nothing worked and I started to be pretty much convinced that it would always be my cross to bear. One day during a conversation with my best friend Dodo, I noticed that when I started a sentence with a vowel, I could continue talking without stuttering as badly. I took this idea and worked with it until I was able to start a conversation without any impediment. It took about a year and a half to work out the kinks, but my life started to improve once again.

Later on, I had a recurrent dream that began when I was a young adult and continued until I was a middle-aged man. The dream about my life or death in a war environment started on a very dark night with no stars or moon. I could see two faint electric lamps on top of wooden poles at each end of the block. The light gave a brownish color to the street and the houses on each side of it.

Then, from across the street came a German soldier dressed in the very recognizable green uniform, helmet, and black boots. He had a machine gun pointed at me as he marched towards me very slowly. As he came closer, the barrel of his machine gun rose toward my head. I was not in any kind of uniform, at least not that I was aware of. At that time, the only thing I had in my hand was a bayonet.

There were no words during my dream, only eye contact. While the German soldier moved slowly toward me, I moved slowly backwards, step by step. During my retreat, I looked frantically for someone to help me. But no one was around and everything was deathly still except for the German coming toward me. I kept thinking that it wasn't fair that I only had a bayonet, while he had a machine gun. I did not mind dying, but at least I wanted a chance to defend myself. As he kept coming forward and I kept backing up, I reached the sidewalk. The house just behind me had a door with a round doorknob. At that point, my thoughts changed. I wondered if I could reach the door before he pulled the trigger.

When I touched the door, my heart started to beat very fast and the anticipation of saving myself was very strong. I held the bayonet in my right hand, while I slowly put my left hand behind my back and hoped that he would not see the move. When my back touched the door, I tried to turn the knob to the left and then to the right, but the knob did not move. I tried to push the door open with my rear end, but nothing happened. At that point, I was close to panic because the German soldier had seen my efforts and slowly started to move his machine gun to his waist. My eyes were fixated on his trigger finger as I watched for any slight movement. Then his finger started very slowly to squeeze the trigger. When the trigger was completely depressed and the bullet ready to escape from the barrel, I suddenly woke up. I was terrified, but relieved to find myself in my own bed.

This dream was part of my life for over twenty-five years. In the beginning, the dream bothered me a lot, but I never tried to have anyone analyze it. Maybe I should have, but for me it was still another by-product of war, like the other PTSD experiences I had.

After a year or two, the dream had become part of me and I subconsciously turned it into a lucid dream. While I was still participating in the dream, I started to feel like I was also a second person witnessing a play. That observer kept saying, "Do not fear. You will not be killed. This is only a dream and you already know the ending." The horrors of the original dream remained, but the lucid dreaming helped me become more able to cope. Thankfully, I have not had this dream in years.

During my many short stays at home, I developed a friendship with three other boys, Jean Louis Montaigu, Nono, and Boucher. We called ourselves the Three Musketeers. Jean Louis moved ten minutes away from our house became Boucher's neighbor. But we all had our bicycles, so Vigneux was our turf.

For me, being home was like having a slice of something good each time. My parents mainly had two families with whom they were friends, the Montaigus and the Michelets. Both families treated me like their own. I spent a lot of my time at the Montaigu's house. My parents visited them on a regular basis and we played a lot of bridge. At that time, I was very good at this card game. I usually teamed up with one of the Montaigus against my mom and dad. It was fun, since it was through bridge that I could belong to two groups, adults and my friends.

I remember one particular Christmas when we had quite a few friends for dinner before bridge. While the help cleared the dishes, I went around the table and drank whatever was left in every wine glass. I felt pretty good after my last glass. After seeing a few of my incontrollable body movements, my parents guessed what I had done and put me to bed. No bridge for me that night.

When I was home, the two people who had the most influence on my life were my mother and Marcel Montaigu. My mother did not baby me. I had my daily chores to do before I could go and enjoy my day. Before I left the house, I had to tell my mom where I would be and when I would be back. She never put any pressure on me. My word was trusted and never did I do anything to change that.

Marcel Montaigu, Mrs. Montaigu's brother, was my special friend. I considered him a much older brother, since at the time he was thirty-five years old, while I was fifteen. When I was home, I visited him at his workplace every Saturday morning. Marcel was a furniture maker and on Saturdays I helped him by doing whatever he needed. Actually, the reason I wanted to be with him was that I could talk to him about anything. At that time, there was nothing more important than seeing Marcel. Looking back at those moments, I realize that he kept me on the right path since I did not dare do anything to disappoint him.

The Montaigus introduced me to camping. Marcel had an enclosed truck in which he put an ice box and a small, propane stove-top. We camped for several weeks at a time, living in tents and having all the comforts in the truck. During one trip, Marcel, his brother, and I went fishing for three days in a row. I walked most of the time, but I did not catch any fish. On our return, I decided that fishing was not for me.

I liked to be inside our tent when it rained. The noise of the droplets on the fabric was very soothing and had a musical rhythm. During rainy days, I enjoyed reading inside the tent. I had a feeling of well-being in this pro-tected environment. Since I played piano, guitar, and accordion, I tried to compose some very basic melodies within the rain's rhythmic patter on the tent. It was fun. Although nothing came of it, trying gave me satisfaction.

The interaction of my family with the Michelets was very much the same as with the Montaigus. Mr. Michelet, an engineer for an American company, was instrumental in my understanding of higher math. He tutored me for six months on a weekly basis. As a result, math became one of my strengths and that seemed to be the push I needed to finish my schooling.

Once when I returned from school, I discovered that we had new neighbors, Mr. and Mrs. Duchene and their two children. I became very good friends with the son, who was about two years younger than I. Mr. Duchene built a machine shop and seemed to be quite busy. To my astonishment, one day while I was on vacation, he asked my father if I could help him. Of course, I was very happy because the work was out-side of my usual intellectual environment. It was also something to do with my hands, which appealed to me.

When I started, I did not even know what a mold was, but very soon I learned how to use the different machines. Surprisingly, I became very good. In fact, I was so good that Mr. Duchene contacted my father and suggested he send me to a professional school to learn the trade. Or course, my father declined, but I still helped occasionally when needed. While it lasted, it opened my mind to the fact that I liked to do things with my hands.

Mr. Duchene had a collection of very old cars. One in particular was a pickup truck with just two seats in front. For turn signals there were two red wooden hands, one on each side. When he was ready to turn, the driver pulled a string attached to the hand he wanted to use. The hand came out horizontal to the road to show which way he was going to turn.

As a teenager, my values were changing. Girls started to look pretty, but I was very shy. My first real interest was Francoise, who lived on the main road not far from our house. Her domicile looked like a little castle with a lot of grounds behind an iron gate. Unfortunately, every time I talked to her, she was in the second-floor window while wishing she were down with me. Somehow, it never happened. For a while we stayed friends at a distance. Then I found other things to do.

One of the sweetest moments of my teenage life occurred when I met my blind friend. He was just turning the corner from my street into the main street when I saw him for the first time. He was all dressed in black and he wore dark glasses and carried a white cane. Without any hesitation, he said, "*Bonjour.*" I wondered how he knew I was across the street. While we were walking to the main plaza, we struck up a conversation. After we introduced ourselves, I learned that he lived in a special place for blind people, but he was here on vacation. He lived a block and a half from our house.

I was very interested in his feelings, since I thought that it would be natural to be depressed and angry because of his condition. To my amazement, he was very happy. He never complained and his words were always positive. I never told him, but he changed my attitude. From then on, I decided I had nothing to complain about in my life. Each time, I remembered the soft voice of my blind friend. When I talked with him, I actually forgot that he was blind.

During my upbringing, my parents always taught me to think about others and to be grateful for what I had. I don't know if the memory of the dead people on Warsaw's streets had anything to do with it, but when I saw a beggar or a person in need, I felt an urge to help if I could. I promised myself that when it became possible later on in my life, I would pay for the operation for my blind friend to see. Little did I know that no operation could restore his sight. At that time, I thought that money could solve almost anything.

Later on when I was in Paris to learn my new trade, I encountered a woman beggar who was missing one leg. Her regular begging spot was in the Place de la Madeleine. Every day, I went out of my way to pass in front of her so I could leave a few francs in her dish. I wanted to do more, but at the time I was not able to. After many months of providing her with a few francs, I promised myself that someday when I was financially able to do so, I would give her enough money so that she would not have to beg anymore.

Several years later, when I returned to Paris from the United States, I went to see if I could find the woman beggar. She was still there and she looked as though I had left her just the day before. With some old friends, I found help for her and I gave her enough money to last at least three years. My friends thought that I was completely crazy, but I did what I had to do and I felt good about it.

To this day, when I see a homeless person, I give money. Maybe the money will go for drugs or wine, but that is not my concern. I do what I feel I have to do. On occasion over the years, I forgot what my parents instilled in me. Each time I was knocked down by life events, and I returned to the real value of life.

Chapter 15

When I was a young boy, I went to England, Spain, and Switzerland many times. The trips that my parents sent me on started in my early childhood. At the time they seemed normal, so I did not pay much attention to them. There are several schools of thought about a young person traveling most of his youth instead of being with his family. Perhaps I could have said I didn't want to go, but my protests probably would have been to no avail. However, I don't think any youngster could have received a better education than I did as I discovered the people, the languages, and the cultures of many other countries.

Three trips remain etched in my mind. The first one began when I came home to Vigneux from school long enough to change suitcases. My mother and I had attended the local church and were friendly with the priest, who was called the *curé*. The church had a summer camp for young boys and I ended up going when I was about 11. I do not remember if I wanted to go. Maybe it was just a continuation of the idea that when I was home, I should go somewhere else. Whatever the reason, I went.

The pastor was a small man. I remember that he always wore a square, black hat and very often sat in a café bar on a high stool while he sipped a glass of red wine. The young priest who helped him was a huge man. At least that is how he looked to me from my young perspective. He was very impressive to me. I remember one time he took two of us, one in each arm, and extended his arms above his head, then asked us how he should deal with us. For a moment, we were not sure if it was a game or not. The young priest was a good person and we were glad he was coming with us.

The summer camp was in Haute Savoie in the northeast part of France, an area with a beautiful mountain range, small rivers, forests, and a lake close to Ancy, a town where we also had fun. The camp ran from July 25 to August 25. The train trip to Haute Savoie took all night. We arrived at 8:30 the next morning. Rereading some of the letters that I wrote to my parents about the trip, I discovered that I carried my own sandwich which I ate during the night. We slept some, but because we all were excited, we could not stop talking.

After the train arrived, we were taken by bus to our camp. It was in a clearing with the forest surrounding us and a small river flowing alongside. Our camp consisted of huge military tents with folding army cots. At the entrance to the camp were two totem poles which I had never seen before. They were made of wood and painted different colors. Later on I was told that I belonged to the Indian tribe, while the cowboys were in another tent. I think I was the only Indian who didn't know about totem poles. People in the United States are often surprised to discover that children in France played cowboys and Indians. American Westerns dubbed in French were our favorite movies.

Our arrival day came without any surprises. We had to organize ourselves to live from our suitcases. We were told the rules and regulations, just like in the army. Then we were given our tin utensils that included a spoon, fork, plate, and a goblet. As usual, I wrote to my parents for a care package. I wanted some fruits and pain *d'epice*, a sweet, spicy bread.

The next morning we were awaken by the *reveille*, the morning bugle corps assembly. After the *reveille*, we went to the river for the morning wash. The water was cold so it was a quick wash. Sometimes when no one was watching, there might have been no wash at all. After the wash, we had assembly and then breakfast. When breakfast was done, we all helped the cook by peeling potatoes. After that chore was finished, we started our cowboy and Indian wars.

Our Indian tribe had a second camp close by in the forest. We even had our own totem pole. Later on, we used the totem pole to tie up our cowboy prisoners. The war rules consisted of having a colored rag attached behind our backs. When we battled the opposition, if we lost the rag, we were considered prisoners. Since the cowboys were looking for us, we were very happy to ambush them in the forest.

One of the priests was a cowboy and one day he became our pris-oner. It was fun to have him as a prisoner. We tied him to our totem pole and we all danced our Indian war dance around him. Then it was time for the cowboys to come and free him before dinner. We thought we were ready for them. I don't remember how they did it, but by the end of the afternoon, the priest was free. We didn't know where he hid until supper. For me, it was a good day of fun.

War between the cowboys and Indians was not our only preoccupa-tion. Ancy was not far, so we all visited that town several times. We went on a boat tour and took advantage of the beach by the lake. It was a nice break from the wilderness.

Back at the camp, we went into the forest and learned about different types of moss, insects, birds, and snails. I also learned about escargots, very big snails which usually come out after the rain. After they are caught and processed, they are eaten. *Escargots de Bourgogne* is a French deli-cacy, even though some people refuse to eat snails. Well prepared with garlic, butter, and white wine, they are a succulent delicacy.

August 25, our last day at camp, came very quickly. It seemed as though we had just arrived and now we had to leave and go back home. Collectively, a feeling of uncertainty engulfed us. We started to talk among ourselves about how we felt about going back home. I found out that some boys did not have much to go back to. As for myself, I realized that it did not matter because I would probably be leaving again soon after my arrival.

After everything was packed, we took the train home. My parents were waiting for me and I was happy to see them, but they were aston-ished how bad I looked. Later on I found out that during my stay in Haute Savoie, I had lost almost thirty pounds. Playing cowboys and Indians often lasted into the nights as we planned our strategies. All the activity with little rest had taken its toll. I looked like a head on a pair of sticks. I stayed at home for a week or so, just long enough to start gaining some weight. Then I headed back to school.

When I was about 14, I went to England because my father had an office in Lion Square in London, as well as friends in Nuneaton, Warwickshire. I remember when I was first in London, I was apprehen-sive about traveling by myself. I mostly did not know where I was going when I had to travel outside the hub, but I loved taking the double-deckers. In London, I took taxis, which I considered very exciting. All the taxis looked the same. They were square and black. The doors opened from the middle of the taxi to the back.

One day I was lost in the middle of the city, so I decided to take a taxi. I jumped into one and very proudly said, "Lion Square please." The taxi did not move. Then the driver opened the window that separates the driver from the passenger and smiled and said, "Young man, you are in Lion Square." Embarrassed and a little confused, I got out and looked up. It was then that I realized I was in front of my father's office.

While I was in London, I went to boarding school for a short while. I was not going to stay in that school, but my parents wanted me to improve my English. I was driven by the office manager every morning. After about two months, my English was much better and I was on the way to Nuneaton, a small town northeast of Warwickshire County. The center of the town had been destroyed during World War II. The town is close to Coventry and Birmingham, two much bigger towns. Coventry is famous for building the famous Jaguar cars.

Nuneaton grew after the war mainly because of its textile industry. I assume that I ended up in Nuneaton because of textiles. Even though I came to England without knowing anyone in London or Nuneaton, I was used to being with people who were new to me, whether they were friends of my father or not.

My dad's friends were the Lloyds. In England that is a famous name because of the Lloyds of London insurance company. However, as far as I know, there was no connection between the two. The Lloyds had two daughters and a son named Joseph. Their house looked almost like a castle, with little towers that stretched from the ground to the roof. The Lloyds had at least half a dozen cars. The sports cars belonging to the daughters were beautiful. They were all convertibles and at my young age, I drooled over them. There was also a Rolls Royce in the garage, but that did not make much of an impact on me, since the sports cars were my heaven.

The daughters were much older than Joseph and I. Both of them had boyfriends who were very nice to me. Of course, I kept dreaming of getting a ride in one of the convertibles, but I was not sure that would ever happen.

The Lloyds had a live-in maid and a cook. The meals were served in the formal dining room. Food at that time was a very important part of my life. I liked to eat whatever I wanted, which sometimes did not work out. For breakfast I was served eggs with what I called lard, but now I know it was bacon. I complained to my parents that I could not eat such a thing. So for breakfast I limited myself to bread and butter.

Little did I know that it was going to get worse. There was a tradition in the family that at four o'clock, everybody gathered in the salon for tea. The maid brought leek sandwiches on sliced white bread, like sandwich bread in the United States. That was a no-no for someone like me who was used to eating crusty baguettes. I decided this must have been the reason the English and French had fought a hundred-year war. To add to this fiasco, everybody watched cricket games, which to this day I have never understood.

My food dilemma was getting difficult to handle. I needed to find a solution. I could not write to my parents for a care package since that would offend the family. The Lloyds owned the Nuneaton public transportation, as well as a dozen confectionary stores which sold all types of ice cream sandwiches, sweets, English and imported chocolate, bottled soft drinks, cakes, and other wonderful foods. The confectionary stores were part of my solution.

Since I could ride the double-deckers for free, I could visit the stores at will. Toward the beginning of my stay, I sometimes went with Joseph so I could learn the town's traffic patterns. After a short while, I was the master of my travels in Nuneaton. Now I must confess that honesty was not my primary concern. When I visited the stores, I could serve and pay by myself. That was the perfect time to perform my dubious maneuver. An ice cream sandwich cost three pence, a gold-colored, multi-edged coin. Instead of paying with a three-pence coin, I dropped in a big one-pence coin which made a lot of noise when it hit the inside of the cashier's drawer. The noise was my way of showing that I had paid for the ice cream bar.

Looking at my action now, I cannot say why I was short-changing the family. It was not lack of money. I am sure that if I had asked, I would have been invited to take whatever I wanted. Maybe I was getting even for those leek sandwiches. Whatever the reason, the confectionary stores solved my hunger problem.

Aside from the food situation, I had a wonderful time with the Lloyds. I did not have any time to get bored. We went to the theater at least twice a week. It was with the family that I discovered stock car racing. We also went to the big port town of Liverpool and to London on a regular basis. I was very impressed because no matter where we went, doors were opened. Mr. Lloyd seemed to be well-known everywhere. Traveling in a Rolls Royce was certainly not a handicap.

On one trip to London, I got all wet. We were across from the Royal Palace in the park. Since I was tired, I sat on the border of a very large fountain. There were a lot of people around waiting for the changing of the guards at Buckingham Palace. I was not paying attention when Joseph sneaked up and scared me. I jumped backward and fell into the fountain. For a moment, I was the most important show in the park. Needless to say, I did not see the changing of the guards that day. When I think about it now, it is a humorous and pleasant memory.

Joseph and I had good times together. I was treated like a brother, not only by his parents, but also by his sisters and their boyfriends. When my time to leave was near, I was given few rides in the sport car. For me, the trip was a complete success after those rides.

When it was time for me to say goodbye, I knew I would never forget the feeling arriving at Heathrow Airport in a Rolls Royce and having someone open the door for me. What a finish!

The next trip I especially remember was when I went to Spain with my mother. At the time I was about 16, and contrary to young people now, I was very happy and not at all ashamed to travel with my mother. We were good friends in addition to being mother and son. Traveling from France to another country was not easy then since there was a ban on exporting money. Of course, since my dad had a business, he could make money transfers from one business entity to another. So my mother and I were soon on our way.

The French train was very comfortable. We were in first class taking advantage of all the perks during our over-night trip to the Spanish border. The steam-engine train had a Pullman wagon where we had a sleeping compartment for the two of us. My mom and I had dinner in the restaurant a few cars down before we retired for the night.

Early the next morning, the train stopped at the frontier and the Spanish immigration agents boarded the train to verify passports. After that stop, we waited for the train to continue the trip into Spain. However, we soon learned that the tracks from France to Spain did not match. It seems that when General Franco took over Spain during the Spanish Civil War, he was afraid that help to his enemies could come from the south of France. Therefore, he decided that all the rail tracks would be one foot wider than the French ones.

So my mother and I were very surprised that we had to leave the train, carry our suitcases, and find a train that was going our way. Looking at it now, it was humorous because we did not know which train to take. We stood on the platform asking questions that no one could answer. One response that I particularly remember was, "Whatever train moves, take it." At the time, the Spanish trains were not on schedule. Even if some had a schedule, it did not mean anything. Our destination was Llansa. From there, we needed to take another means of transportation. After much discussion with the native people, we took a local train that stopped at all stations. At least we knew for sure that it was going to Llansa.

The train ride was an unforgettable experience. I was overwhelmed by the cacophony of sounds and smells. Since it was a local train everybody and their relatives were on it, along with live chickens in huge baskets, rabbits in cages, and enough food to feed an army: sausage, cheese, bread, and much more. Everybody had sandwiches and since we looked like tourists, we were offered food and drink. It was the first time that I saw wine in a *gourda*, a leather pouch from which everybody drank. The end that the liquid came from was made of a sculpted horn, so no mouths touched it. I don't remember how long it took us to reach Llansa, but time was not a concern because the trip was so interesting.

From Llansa we had to go to Puerto de la Selva. When we finished gathering our luggage, the chase for a taxi started. We found one not too far from the train station. At last we were on our way to our final destination. To reach Puerto de la Selva, we had to drive through a part of the Costa Brava, which was a hair-raising experience.

The road, even though paved, had two very narrow lanes with nothing to prevent a car from rolling down the side of the mountain. The road was just a long zig-zag. There were no straight lines between the turns, but our driver was completely fearless. He drove with one hand on the wheel while the other was busy waving hello to all the people he encountered. Sitting in the back seat, my mother and I held hands to give each other some support. We were not sure that Puerto de la Selva would see us.

After few hours, we reached our hotel and the place was beautiful. We were by the sea. The salt smell was great. The beach touched the hotel. On the other side, small fishing boats were tied down. The hotel was a small one, and when we were shown our room, it was just perfect. Half of the room was above the waterline. From the window, any brave person could have dived into the sea.

The hotel had a small restaurant. We had a very nice waitress who tried to converse in French while I tried my Spanish. The service included the choice of going at midmorning to greet the fishing boats and choose our fish for lunch or dinner. For me, being at Puerto de la Selva was a big change since the town was small and it was my first time by the sea.

It was quiet during the day. Swimming in the sea was perfect and lying on the sandy beach was delightful. The mountains were within walking distance from our hotel, so my mother and I took sandwiches and water and went hiking.

During this trip I found out that the Spanish people have a very different way of managing their time. At night, no one ate before ten o'clock. The afternoons were more like France since almost everything was closed from one o'clock to about four. Then business resumed until about eight in the evening.

After dinner, the entertainment started. I was introduced to a dance called the *Sardaña* with the band on the beach while everybody danced. This went on until dawn, but Mom and I went to bed much earlier. Astonishingly, people who spent all night dancing were at work early in the morning. I wondered how they could do that. When I tried that later on in Lyon, I crashed.

After relaxing for a short time in Puerto de la Selva, I started to feel very sleepy. No matter what time of the day, I suddenly fell asleep. I even fell asleep while eating. One time my head fell into the plate I had in front of me. This lasted for about a week and I did not have any control over it. I did not see the doctor at the time. We assumed that my condition was just fatigue.

After a while, we were joined in Spain by our friends Mr. and Mrs. Montaigu, and Mrs. Montaigu's brother, Marcel. Years later when I read letters that my mother wrote to my father, I found out that the trip was a therapeutic trip after all I had been through. My father always asked how I was doing and what my reactions were while on the trip. I found out that the Montaigus joined us for my benefit. Recently, when I learned about narcolepsy, I wondered if my sudden falling asleep had been another symptom of Post Traumatic Stress Syndrome.

When I felt better, the five of us decided to rent a car to go to Barcelona for few days. It was a very nice trip, but at the hotel we were warned about the *carabineros,* General Franco's military police. We were told that they could stop anyone for any reason, so we should have all our papers in order. Barcelona is a beautiful town and also a big port. I loved the town, not only for its display of beauty, its parks, and its buildings, but also for the flamenco music. In addition, they had one of my preferred soccer teams. I remember picking up an annoying habit while we were traveling in Spain. At that time there were no tissues, so I kept small handkerchiefs in my pocket. Restaurants provided cloth napkins as small as my handkerchiefs. Every time we ate in a restaurant, I found a napkin in my pocket afterwards.

After exploring Barcelona, we all went to Madrid. The two-lane road leading into Madrid meandered through a not-so-nice view. There was the smell of garbage and Madrid was behind a wall. It was astonishing for me because it was not how I imagined the entrance to the city. However, once we were inside, it was very nice.

During the Spanish trip I was introduced to different, good foods. I discover calamari, a member of the octopus family. I ate fish everyday, yet it was never prepared the same way. The music, the food, and the environment were fantastic. After almost a month in Spain, we all returned together by train. For me, it was a fantastic trip. I saw, I ate, I heard, and I smelled things that I had never encountered before. Now it was time to go back home and then off to school. I knew I would have good memories for long time to come.

Part Two

TALENTS
TRAVAILS
TRIUMPHS

Chapter 16

The images here, like the memories in the other chapters, reflect my remembrance of times that are divided between the good and the not-so-good.

The Polish passport with photographs of my mother and me has its own story. So do the other images that highlight my life. My favorite is the drawing of the giraffe and the little boy. My mom sketched that in a letter she sent me when I was in boarding school. She never explained its meaning, but I think that she wanted me to know that I could become as tall as the giraffe if I wanted to.

Even now, I enjoy looking at these images because they keep telling me a story I never want to forget, a story seen through my eyes...

My mother and I

Soon after we were at this Berlin beach frequented by the Nazi elite, my mother and I found ourselves on the train to Auschwitz.

*My mother was required to carry this identification with her
at all times when she lived in Poland. The Germans added the
stamp at the bottom.*

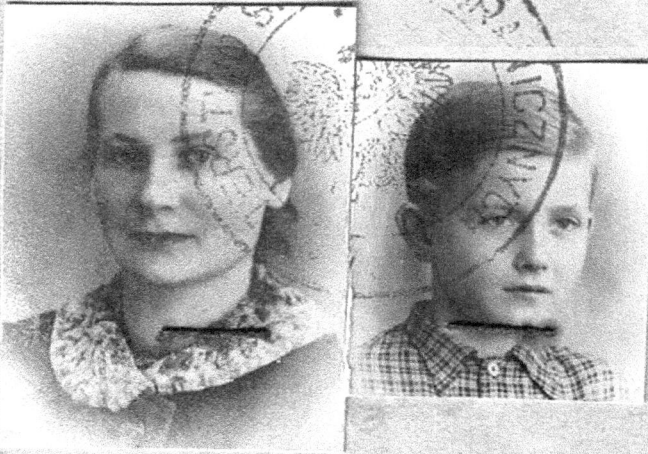

3

Fotografie – Photographies

Podpis posiadacza
Signature du porteur

*My mother and I found safety in Sweden after our escape
from Poland.*

My parents gave me this bicycle on our first Christmas in Vigneux.

lundi 18 octobre

ma chère maman je bésion de la Peintu[re]
et du Papier a lettre et encor Pot de colle
blanche avec un Pinso sé Pesion Pour e l'eca[...]
Je me Porte bien et Pour noéle je Prepa[re]
un Joli Pelites Journale el i y a des Jolis des[...]
je travaills bien et je me Plaioroth
et je vou dré qué tu manvoi un livre
Pour Pindre des decouPage et je vouDré q[...]
tu men voi le livre de dinbo dans cele e Joine
on va Faire une maison en carton ou Pail[...]
des désin des arbre et a Prai on calle
sur brin au simoire Je vous embrasse bien f[...]

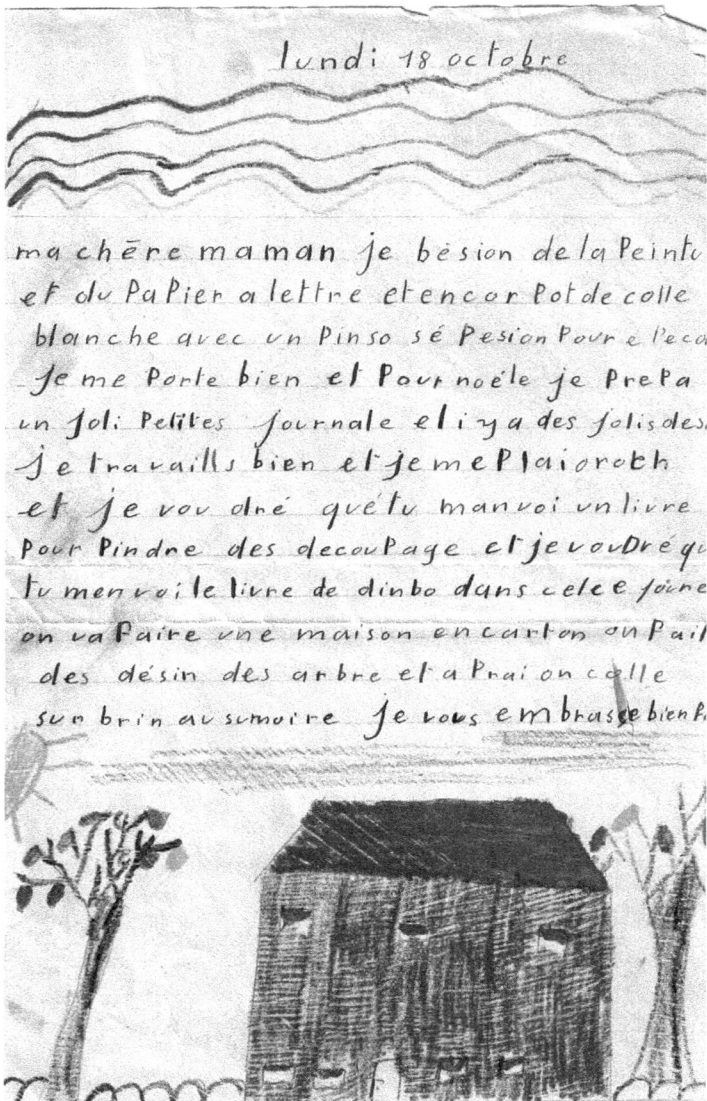

*One of the many "begging" letters I wrote to my parents when I was
learning French.*

My mother drew this sketch of me looking at the giraffe — and
included it in a letter she wrote to me.

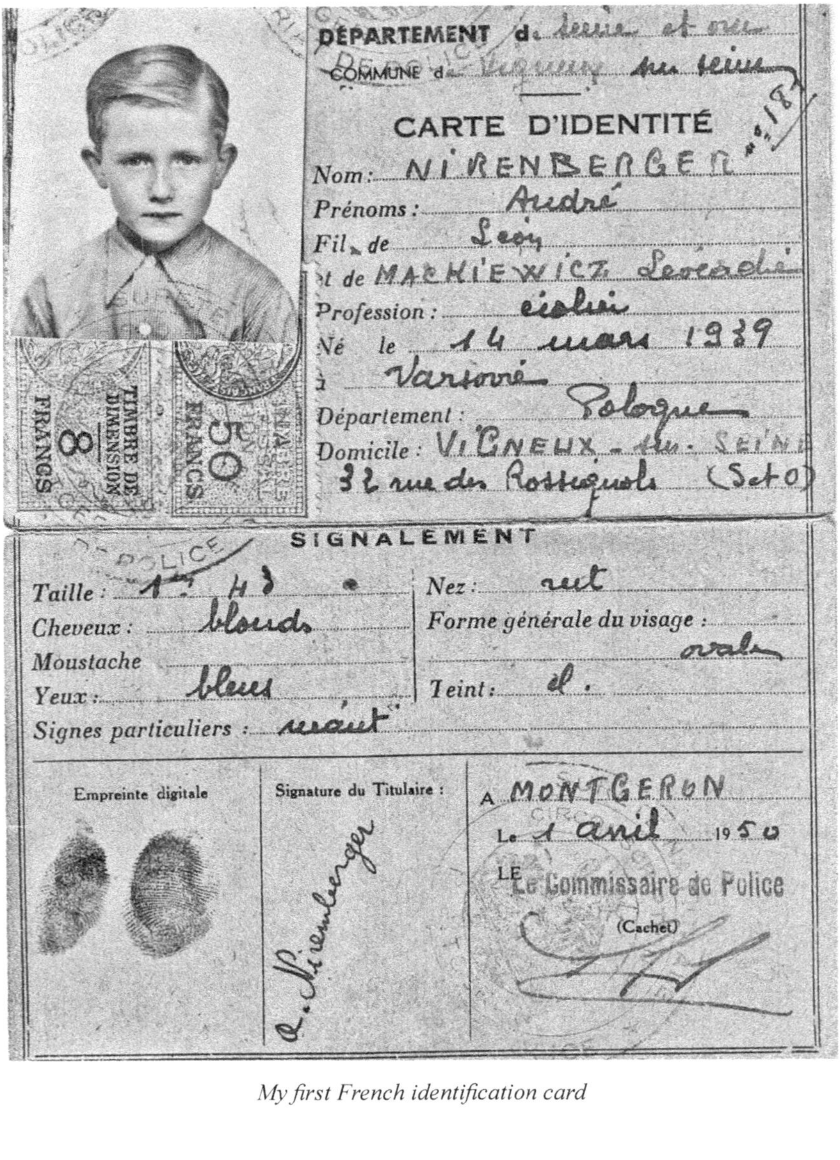
DÉPARTEMENT de Seine et Oise
COMMUNE de Vigneux sur Seine

CARTE D'IDENTITÉ

Nom: NIRENBERGER
Prénoms: André
Fils de Léon
et de MACHIEWICZ Léocadie
Profession: écolier
Né le 14 mars 1939
à Varsovie
Département: Pologne
Domicile: VIGNEUX-sur-SEINE
32 rue des Rossignols (S et O)

TIMBRE DE DIMENSION 8 FRANCS
50 FRANCS

SIGNALEMENT

Taille: 1m 43
Cheveux: blonds
Moustache
Yeux: bleus
Signes particuliers: néant
Nez: rect
Forme générale du visage: ovale
Teint: cl.

Empreinte digitale
Signature du Titulaire:
A MONTGERON
Le 1 avril 1950
Le Commissaire de Police
(Cachet)

My first French identification card

*I received my First Communion at L'eglise
St. Pierre in Vigneux.*

I began my career as a hairstylist in Paris.

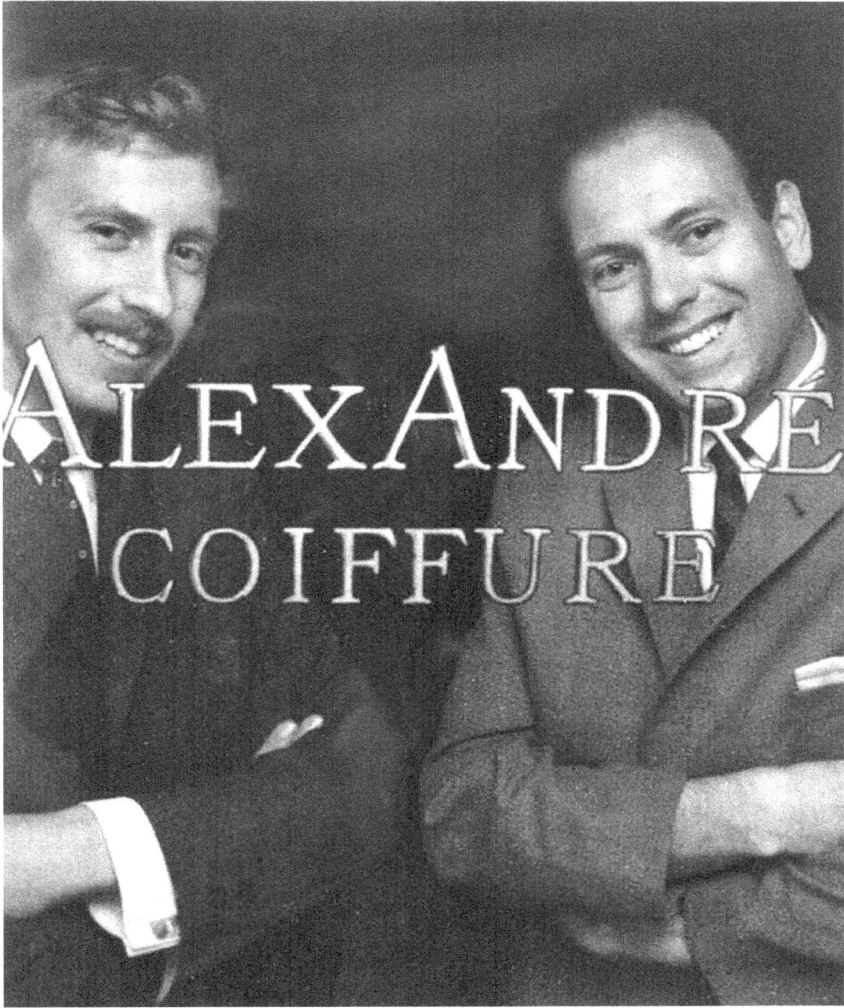

Grand opening of AlexAndré Coiffure on Chicago's Gold Coast

My mother and I enjoyed my first American car, a 1960 Chevrolet Impala.

Carolina III and I were married on May 15, 1971.

Chapter 17

With all that education behind me and with the paper to prove it, my parents hoped that I would become a person of stature. Perhaps like Mr. Floriot, a real-life French Perry Mason. Or maybe like my cousin Oleg, an economist with three books to his name. However, in my heart I knew that the intellectual life was not for me. I had received my Master's in Marketing at the Sorbonne, but I still wasn't sure what I wanted to do with my life.

Therefore, I decided to give my dad's idea a try. Even though he never involved me directly with my possible role in his textile operations, it was understood at that time in Europe that everyone entering a business would begin at the apprenticeship level. So one bright morning my dad and I went to his office at Chatillon Mouly Roussel. I don't know when my father started the business, but I know that his older brother Joseph was involved at the beginning in Warsaw, where the business was called Primavera. The Germans confiscated Primavera when the war started, but at that time my father was in France overseeing his factories there.

Chatillon Mouly Roussel produced and sold high fashion textiles, as well as some of the more basic materials like taffeta and simple satin. Most of the grand couturiers in Paris purchased their textiles from my father's business. He also supplied private tailors. At the time, most everyone in Europe had suits made.

The philosophy that my father used to expand his business in many countries was to establish partnerships with other investors. As a result, my dad had a different partner in each country. His Swedish partner, Mr. Josephson, helped my mother and me escape from Poland during the war. Sometimes, the demand for fashion fabrics was greater than my father's companies could supply, so he had other factories produce textiles for him. Most of those factories were in Morocco in North Africa.

In Paris, my dad's office was on the second floor of a four-story building. An old iron-work elevator stopped at an iron door. From there, we could see the telephone operator. The floor was an old parquet that squeaked under each step. Later on, I found out that everybody could recognize my father's footsteps and they were the signal to get busy. My dad's office was a large, triangular room with windows overlooking two streets. One was Avenue de L'Opera. The opera house was just one block away. From one of the windows, I could see Le Cadrant, a café where my mom and I sometimes waited for my father.

I stayed in the office for several hours that first day. What impressed me was that my father knew everything by heart. When anyone came to ask for any information about anything to do with color, material quality, customers, or anything else, he answered without hesitation. He never looked at a book or a record.

I was impressed. All of a sudden, I was seeing a man I did not know. This person was no longer just my father. I felt a certain respect that I had never experienced before. During those few hours, I just observed. I did not say anything unless I was introduced to people who came to his office.

Finally a man came to his office and I found to my surprise that I was not going to work with my dad after all. Instead, I was going to work in another of his buildings in Paris where the rolls of textiles came from the factory to be inspected for imperfections. This was to be my first apprentice foothold in my father's business. My new boss was an older man who smoked a pipe and wore glasses. He had a big nose, one of those sometimes the result of indulging oneself in drink. He was the supervisor of all the employees in the second building.

Of course, since I was completely green in the work place, my initiation was about to start. It did not matter that I was the son of the owner. I was treated like an apprentice, which meant that I did not know anything and I was open for a good laugh. One morning, my boss asked me to get a certain pair of scissors. I ended going to many departments and each person told me the scissors were in the next one. After making the tour, I realized what had happened and it all ended in fun. From then on, I was accepted as one of them.

My first job was to observe how to inspect the rolls of textile. After the big, heavy roll was brought to one end of a large table, a thick wooden stick was put through the middle of the roll. Then two people on either side of the table pulled the material over the flat table and unfolded it. The factory roll was three feet wide, but when the workers unfolded the fabric, it turned out to be six feet wide. With each pull of the textile, the two people went over the material. If an imperfection were found, they marked it on the side with a colored yarn. I had to observe for several days before I tried my hand at it.

I stayed in that position about two months, but never became very proficient. Instead of firing me, my dad decided to send me to one of his factories in Lyon in south of France. At the same time, I would start attending textile engineering school. Once again, I would be away from home. All the arrangements were made within a few days. Mr. Merendol, who was in charge of all the Lyon operations, found lodging for me in a room at an older lady's apartment in an area called Croix Rousse. I slept there and had breakfast at her place. The factory was not very far away.

The first day arrived without any fanfare. I was introduced as a new worker and I met my two bosses. The person running the factory was a woman. I found later that her nickname was The Witch. My immediate boss was a mechanic. In the textile trade, he was called a *gareure*. For the first few weeks, day in and day out, I sat on a small, wooden stool with a bucket full of turpentine and cleaned parts for the *métiers*, the machines that wove the material. During this job, I learned the names of all the parts and where they fit on the machines. After one month I was promoted. Now I followed the mechanic and brought him the parts that he needed to repair broken *métiers*.

I also went to the textile engineering school in the mornings. There I was introduced to all types of new technology dealing with textiles. It was interesting, but for some reason, I was not excited about it. While in school, my preferred time was the recess. There were two pianos in the hall where some of us played popular songs and tunes.

I was also busy developing a social life which took more and more of my time. My social life included a girl friend, of course. I also enjoyed meeting with a lot of students in a café close to my pad. The café was also the center for the town's professional soccer team. I was part of that team. We took all our meals at the café. Dancing during the night was a normal thing to do. The bottom line was that there was hardly any time for work or school. It was a good life for a while. When money was short, I found an excuse to write to my dad so he could take care of my financial needs.

Meanwhile, I was promoted to work on one of the machines with another worker. Most of the people working on the *métiers* were women. I learned how to make different knots to repair the thread when it broke. The noise in the factory was very loud. To make ourselves heard, we needed to scream. After working on the machines for a while, I was moved again. This time I worked in the department that dyed the threads before they were woven. I must say, there was a very good effort by management to attempt to educate me at an accelerated pace. But I had no interest in the skills they were teaching me.

Instead, my very important social life was taking over. I started not to go to my pad, so I went to school and then to work without sleep. After a while, I started to sleep in the factory locker room. No one snitched on me for a long time. But my debonair life ended abruptly after few months. The Witch ended my sleeping in the locker room and Mr. Merendol announced to me that I was fired. Of course, he couldn't have done that without first consulting with my father.

Few days later, I was back at home. Surprisingly, my dad did not seem angry, but I found out later that he was disappointed in me. Even though I was an adult, I could still talk with my mother much more freely than I could with my dad. After all, I had spent most of the war years with her before we were reunited with my father in France when I was nine. My mother and I decided to find out what I really wanted to do with my life without any pressure of having to please my dad.

I liked to do things with my hands and I liked fashion. One of my parents' best friends was Pierre Jacy, one of the best-known hairstylists, not only in Europe, but also in the world. He had salons all over Europe, as well as in New York at the Waldorf Astoria, in Palm Beach, in Acapulco, and in Mexico City. Mr. Jacy was involved in the fashion industry. He was also half Polish and half Romanian, another plus.

I decided to be involved in fashion by becoming a hairstylist. In Europe this was an artistic trade that could also be glamorous. It appealed to me and few weeks later I began hairstyling school. The curriculum was very interesting. We had to learn fashions from the time of the French kings, including the famous coifs of Marie Antoinette and Madame Pompadour. We had to familiarize ourselves with the wigs of the period and learn how colors were used then. We also had to develop dexterity in using the hot iron to produce historical hairdos.

This trade in France and throughout Europe is very different from perceptions in the United States. Besides the school's teachers, the most famous French hair designers came to teach us. For the first time, I was truly interested in a trade. It was fun because I could see the potential for expressing myself in an artful medium. I found out that I liked people and I considered glamour appealing.

To my surprise, I was told I was good, and that felt great. At last, people were recognizing some talent in me. Suddenly, I dove into this art milieu that also brought me closer to fashion. I attended Paris fashion shows in which my father was also a participant and very often a producer. I rubbed elbows with the French couturiers.

After two years of schooling, everybody had to enter hair styling contests in all the disciplines in order to graduate. The grading was done by six of the most famous hair artists in France. Pierre Jacy was one of them. When all was done, the best student was given an interview with some of the biggest artists. Gaining a position with them would certainly be glamorous.

Since my father and Pierre Jacy were good friends, they decided when I started hair-styling school that I would eventually work with him. However, it was not going to be easy. Anyone who wanted a job with him first had to do his daughter's hair. That may sound easy, but she had the finest hair in the world and no hair style would hold for any length of time. Early one morning I arrived at the main store on the Rond Point des Champs Elysee, which is situated between the Concorde and the Arc de Triomphe. This is the most glamorous boulevard in France and the people are just as glamorous.

The store had three stories, including the basement. Upon entering, the customer looked at the huge and beautiful perfume department. On the right were the women's stations. On the left was the area for men. Other facilities for both women and men were on the second floor, including massage, make-up, tanning, and more.

The smell was fantastic. The bustle had a very pleasant rhythm. But suddenly I was brought back to earth. I was standing in front of Pierre Jacy and his daughter. Oops! I knew what was coming, but for the first time in my life, I felt very sure of myself. I knew that her hair was not going to defeat me and it did not. That afternoon she told me that I would start the next day. She said that my work on her hair was the best ever.

I was very excited and scared at the same time, because I would be dealing with customers. If they are not happy, my head could roll. I was both apprehensive and happy. Another surprise awaited me the next day. When I showed up for work, I was told to take the second chair from the door. That meant I was the second chair, just like in an orchestra hierarchy which includes the first violinist and then the second one. It also meant that the first chair and I would get the most important clientele. Since there was already a *Monsieur André* on the men's side, I became professionally *Monsieur Alex*. During my time with Pierre Jacy, I styled hair for movie stars, like Suzanne Pleshette and Bridget Bardot and others, as well as for ambassadors' wives and dignitaries from Paris.

My life was fantastic. I was receiving recognition. I was chosen, along with others, to do hair styles for models at fashion shows. I was also one of the lucky ones selected to do models' hair for the French *Vogue* magazine. Life was good. But make no mistake: it was hard to maintain consistency in both creativity and quality. In Europe when people went to a hair designer, they did not tell him what to do. A woman might come to a particular artist who then had the responsibility to give her what best complemented her face, her body, and her personality.

Pierre Jacy had a profound influence on the rest of my life. In the beginning, he was after me all the time to ensure that I performed to his standards. One evening I was so tired of his being after me that I hid on the second floor hoping he would not find me. But I was mistaken. When he saw me, he cornered me. He grabbed my tie with his left hand shook a big finger in front of my nose. My knees were playing castanets.

With a deep voice he said, "André, why don't you do as I tell you?" With a feeble voice I answered, "I am trying. I am trying." He responded, "As of today, you will stop trying and start doing." What a simple strategy! I put it into practice and I know how well it works. I have told this story to many people hoping it might help open some avenues. Maybe it did. I don't know. But I do know that Pierre Jacy's response has guided me through my entire life.

After several months, Pierre Jacy called me to his office. With trepidation, I went. To my surprise, he asked me to sit down and have lunch with him. He always had lunch in his basement office. He questioned me about my business philosophy and travels. By the end of lunch, he told me that my next job was to oversee his other salons in France and in foreign lands. My new position sounded fantastic. Besides the travel, I would meet a lot of very nice people, both important and not-so-important people. Most of all, I would be going to many different countries and I would learn to appreciate a variety of views and ways of thinking. I was absolutely astonished by Pierre Jacy's offer and I could not say anything but yes. I had two weeks to prepare.

Of course, everything has both negative and positive sides. Along with my new responsibilities, I knew I would miss the good times I had with my colleagues. On a regular basis, we met at a sidewalk café called Café de la Paix, located at the corner of Avenue de L'Opera and Boulevard de la Madeleine. Actually it is said to be at the Place de L'Opera. Café de la Paix is where the Parisian haute society assembled to socialize. It was great to relax by sitting along the sidewalk and looking at people passing by. Of course, at the time we were more interested in looking at nice young girls. Sitting there sipping a *café* or a *diabolo menthe*, which is soda with mint syrup, we exchanged stories about the day's work. It was a very friendly atmosphere that held a lot of importance for me.

I also had to stop all other activities I participated in, including soccer, where I played at the highest level for a time. Our games were on Sundays, so on Saturday nights I lay on my bed in the dark with my eyes closed. Then I reviewed the upcoming game in my mind as I thought it would develop. I went through the motions of the game in my mind many times. On the day of the game, I felt as though I were playing it a second time. I knew what to do because I had already visualized it.

Several years ago in the United States, scientists conducted a study about the value of focusing one's mind on a task ahead of time. The study included three groups of professional basketball players who were practicing shooting free throws. One group practiced on the basketball court. The second practiced the free throws in their minds. The third group made no special preparation. The second group improved the most. When I learned about the study, I felt good because I realized that I had been way ahead of my time when I played soccer.

Giving up my friends and my activities was hard. For some reason my life seemed to be going at a certain speed and I did not have any control of it. I was moving again. For a while at least, I would be living out of a suitcase. I was not complaining, but I was apprehensive about the unknown.

On the positive side, I was elated that Pierre Jacy's company had stores in Mexico since I was a buff of Mexican folklore, music, and language. When I was going to school, Mexico seemed to be a far-away land that could never be reached. Now my trip to paradise was about to become a reality. I was going to Mexico for one week. I felt like a little kid who had just been offered his most-wanted toy.

Pierre Jacy's company had two stores in Mexico, one in the Hilton in Mexico City, and the other at the Pierre Marquez in Acapulco. The Pierre

Marquez was situated on a mountain overlooking Acapulco Bay. It was a beautiful site. Both hotels catered to a sophisticated clientele and my job was to ensure that we were providing the same type of service. When I returned to Paris, I was probably the best promoter of Mexico. My trip strengthened my resolve to move to the United States, since it was closer to Mexico than Europe was.

Another exciting adventure came during my first trip to the United States. Pierre Jacy had a salon on the ocean liner *S.S. Liberté* which sailed from Le Havre, France, to Portsmouth, England, and from there to New York Harbor. After packing my suitcase again and bidding my parents *au revoir*, I took the train to Le Havre. This was the first time in my life that I would be sailing on a ship across the sea. I was both excited and apprehensive.

The Pierre Jacy salon on the *S.S. Liberté* was beautiful. It had all the facilities of the larger store on the Rond Point des Champs Elysee. The perfumery was a store in itself. We had place for five hair stylists, along with the two people who took care of the perfume counter and gifts. The whole set-up was just gorgeous.

Our quarters were on the lowest deck where I could hear the engines. It was not fancy, but at the time I did not care. I was just awed at going to the United States and by being in charge. My cabin had two bunk beds. However, no one was sleeping in the cabin with me. I had a porthole through which I could see the water. My ignorance about traveling by sea was evident within a day. The first night was so beautiful that I decided to open the porthole before I fell asleep. During the night, I was awakened by a sloshing noise inside the cabin. After a quick investigation, I found that seawater had come through the porthole that I had left open. My shoes and everything else on the floor were swimming from side to side with the ship's movement. So much for my first night as a sailor!

The ocean liner had three classes: first, second, and third. The passengers could not switch classes. Again I was lucky, because the management gave me a key that enabled me to switch from one class to another. I was amazed at how busy we were during the trip. Only at night after we closed everything could we enjoy ourselves. I liked to stand on the foredeck where the wind brushed my face. I felt as though I were going to a place no one else could go. It was nice and quiet. I felt like I could touch the shining stars. It was a wonderful feeling that I had never experienced before.

The trip to New York took five days. Those were five very busy days for us. After the second day I no longer heard the engines. I made friends with the crew and at night I ate with them. It was so much easier because their dining room was on the same deck as our cabins.

The fourth night after we closed, I was told that at 5 a.m. we would be entering New York Harbor. I had been waiting for this for years. I did not sleep that night so I would not miss anything. With my key, I let myself onto the upper deck in front of the boat. What a beautiful show unfolded!

I could see the skyscrapers on in the horizon and my heart started to beat faster. Even though they were far away, they were very impressive. I had never seen such tall buildings. It was very early in the morning and I was alone, so the enjoyment was all mine. The sea smelled wonderful. I could hear the water splashing against the hull and see the seagulls flying above my head. Then the *piece de resistance* came into view on my left. The Statue of Liberty was so impressive that I had goose bumps. When I was in school, I had learned about the Lady, but I could not believe that I was so close to her. By now, people were out on the decks and I could hear the "Oh's" and the "Ah's" generated by the fantastic view.

Little did I know that another surprise was waiting for all of us. When the ship was a short way from the docks, boats from the New York Fire Department came out and gave us a grand welcome by providing a water-spout honor guard along with a lot of tooting and whistling. Later I discovered that the *S.S. Liberté* had broken the Atlantic crossing record.

It took several hours for the ship to dock and for everyone to disembark. The ship was staying in New York for a few days, so after I took care of business at the Waldorf Astoria salon, I visited the town over the three-day weekend. The salon was just perfect. The stylists were all from France and Italy, everybody was fluent in English, and the clientele was *la creme* of New York. From time to time, I wondered if I were dreaming or just plain lucky to be associated with this milieu.

On Friday night, a friend and I decided to go into town to visit a restaurant called the Three Six on top of a skyscraper. The view of Manhattan was beautiful. I was astonished. Compared to Europe, everything was so much bigger. The cars, the buildings, even the people looked impressive. Lights of all colors shone in the dark night, there was soft music piped in, and the bar looked very friendly. While we sat at the bar sipping our drinks, we talked in French. Not far away was a middle-aged couple who must have overheard our conversation. They asked us if we were French, and after a few more drinks, they invited us to spend the weekend at their place. In 1958, people were nice so we did not have any reason to refuse such an opportunity. My fairy tale was continuing. The couple had a Mercedes Benz and they took us to their house on the Hudson River. When we went back to town two days later, I did not know what to believe. Were all Americans that nice or were we just lucky?

My first purchase in New York was from the Gamble store where I bought sun glasses for my parents and myself. Of course, I could not leave New York without seeing the Rockettes at Radio City Music Hall. I had never seen so many beautiful girls in one place. As I explored the city, I was surprised by the clothes people wore. They did not seem fashionable since the colors didn't match. Some of the women wore odd, shiny hats of all colors. I was definitely looking at a different fashion.

The experiences I had in New York were gratifying. I had seen many European countries and I thought they were all about the same. The traditions might have been a little different, but the look, size, and feeling were very similar. In New York everything was very different. The crowds seemed to be indifferent to who was who and to what people were wearing. There was a feel of personal freedom that I liked.

Alas, it was finally time to leave, but I did not mind since I knew I would soon be returning on the same ship. I made that round trip five times. During one crossing, I took time to consider my future. I remembered the long-ago day when I sat on our doorstep in Vigneux and read two life-changing articles in *Selection,* the French *Reader's Digest*. One article taught me about self-control. The other introduced me to the wonders of the United States and I decided then that I would live there someday. I had already begun to make contacts that would help me fulfill that dream, but first Pierre Jacy had some new plans for me. I was being transferred once again.

Chapter 18

When I returned from my last crossing of the Atlantic, Pierre Jacy decided that I would take care of his stores in many parts of Europe. It was a great opportunity for me to continue to work in a very sophisticated environment throughout France, Germany, Italy and Switzerland. Cities included Paris, Deauville, Biarritz, Megeve, Alpe D'Huez, Juan-les Pins, Nice, La Baule, and Cannes.

Since I was young and recognized in the trade, I was always looking for a good offer even though I had decided to move to the United States. I thought that keeping my options open was a good idea. I had already been corresponding for about six months with a man I'll call Georges who wanted me to work in his salons in the Chicago area.

I was again living out of a suitcase, coming home long enough to say hello and get my laundry done. Seldom did I sit with my friends to have a drink in our café as before. My position was exciting and I liked it. But, of course, now I wanted more.

Few months later while I was traveling, I received an offer from a very influential beauty corporation located in Beirut, Lebanon. It was an offer to be taken seriously and one that needed to be investigated. Since I was in the beauty business, I had learned how to look for the important aspects of all offers. Beirut in the 1950's was considered a second Paris in terms of fashion, style, and taste. The women in particular were very fashionable and knowledgeable about what was in style. The offer looked very good, because if I accepted it, I would be the principal fashion director for the corporation.

The temptation was very strong. However, I felt that somehow I would be betraying the promise I had made to myself a long time ago to move to the United States. I tried to delay my decision, although I was perfectly aware that I already knew the solution. The need to make decisions was coming very fast and I felt as though I were leaping over a wall without having time to see what was on the other side. I felt as though I were making decisions while I was coming down on the still-unknown side. I continued to travel and visit Pierre's salons until I received an ultimatum from Beirut. I decided not to accept the position and I felt good about it.

Now I had a bigger problem on my hands. How would I tell my parents and Pierre Jacy that I had decided to leave and move to the United States? I suspected my parents knew that someday I would be moving because I had been dropping hints for a long time. In fact, when I mustered the strength to tell them, they were not surprised, and at first they were even encouraging. I started to talk to my friends about making the trip to the United States. When I mentioned Chicago, they told me about Al Capone and his gang. They said that I would need a gun to be safe. Of course, they were joking.

As for Pierre Jacy, I had to be more careful because I needed to use my special traveling card that permitted me to travel to the United States and back without any questions from immigration authorities in either country. My next trip was to the United States embassy in Paris. I really did not have a plan besides asking for a visa. I must say that I discovered that I did not know much about immigration law. I knew that to emigrate to the United States, a two-year waiting period was in effect. However, in my ignorance, I thought that because of my travels to that country, I would not have any problems. I was wrong and not very happy.

My trip to the embassy was successful only because I made a daring move. I was directed to a vice consul's office where I presented my reasons for going to the United States. Since I had learned about the conditions for entering the country, I decided to ask for a vacation visa. Then when I was inside, I would play by ear. Little did I know that the vice consul knew about my travels to the United States, so I could not convince him that vacations were my main objective. It was my first experience trying to communicate with a high-level bureaucrat.

When the meeting ended, I did not have a visa. I knew I needed to come up with a second plan before leaving the embassy, so I decided to go to the next vice consul's office without being invited. He probably thought I was his next client. He asked me to sit down and we talked about my visa. He was much younger than the first man and probably not as experienced. I told him the same story and to my surprise, I received a vacation visa good for six months. I left the embassy as quickly as I could before he changed his mind.

Now the hard part was to tell Pierre Jacy that within thirty days, I would no longer be working for him. I was torn between my friendship and the gratitude that I had towards everything he had done for me. However, I had to do it. On Monday morning I went to see him in his basement office. I told him about an opportunity that I had in the United States that I could not refuse. I was trying to make it a long story when he stopped me and said, "I know. I was waiting for you. Good luck and don't forget what I taught you." I was astonished and thankful at the same time. Now I was ready to prepare for my trip to the United States. I could not believe that the decision I had made many years ago was coming to fruition

Now I had even more decisions to make. I didn't even know what I should take with me. This was not like going on vacations to other countries and having my mother pack my suitcase. Now I was responsible for everything. At the time it did not seem important, because I was so excited to be in the middle of my future.

After things settled down, I started to think about all that I would be leaving behind: my parents, my friends, probably a good future in sports, and certainly a secure future in my profession. However, at the time, nothing seemed to be that important. No one could dissuade me from leaving. I was indestructible.

I had two weeks to put all my affairs in order. I decided to see my friends and spend some time reminiscing about the good times we'd had together. I noticed that the closer the departure date, the calmer I became. The frenzy was slowing down. I started to pay more attention to things around me. Realization that I was leaving for good was sinking in. I spent the last few days with my parents, but I do not remember what we talked about. Probably the feelings were very similar to when I was leaving for any other trip.

Then the day arrived. My parents gave me a ride to Orly, which at the time was the main Paris airport. I was traveling on TWA. I had a special affection for the TWA because when I was a young boy, I had watched the planes flying high over our house before going on to land at Orly.

At the airport, my parents walked with me to the plane. It was a four-engine propeller plane that had a big ladder on wheels leaning against the big bird. The only thing that I remember now is my father saying while we walked towards the plane, "I will see you back soon." We must not have been in very good mood, because instead of my saying something nice, I did not respond. Instead, I muttered to myself, "Over my dead body." At the time I did not pay attention to what I was saying to myself. However, later on I regretted it because even though he did not hear it, he certainly did not deserve that from me.

I sat by the small window in the plane and I waved, not knowing if they knew where I was. The engines roared, the plane started to move, and at that moment I realized that I had just exchanged security for insecurity. Getting comfortable in my seat, I thought to myself, "It is my choice."

My first stop in the United States was Detroit. At the time, it was the port of entry for some of the passengers. Since my port of entry was Chicago, I had to get off the plane and was ushered into a room where I was to stay until the plane was ready to board again. At eight o'clock the next morning I landed at Chicago's O'Hare Airport. After I found my suitcases, immigration was next. Fortunately, I answered all the questions right and America was in front of me.

My destination in the Chicago suburbs was Evanston. My new boss Georges picked me up at the airport. The drive from O'Hare to Evanston went through Skokie, a heavily Jewish neighborhood. I was fascinated by the buildings bordering the road. They all looked like the buildings I had seen in Westerns with Gary Cooper and John Wayne. They were one-story tall had and flat roofs. The only difference was the material used to build them. In the movies they were made of wood, while the ones in Skokie were made of bricks.

The landscape surprised me. Everything was so new and exciting. Unlike New York's tall buildings, it was very flat and spread out with very large streets. Another change I had to get use to fast were the stop signs. Compared to the stop signs in Europe, the laws here were more complicated. During the ride I did not have much of a conversation with my new boss because my head was bobbing from left to right, taking in all that I could. When our car entered Evanston, the scenery changed again. Now I noticed tall trees, beautiful greenery, and a small but very attractive park with benches. I was impressed.

Finally we arrived at the place that would be my domicile for some time. Once again, I could not believe what I was seeing. When I was in school, I had learned about the Great Lakes, but I could not imagine a lake that I could not see across. Now I was going to live two blocks from Lake Michigan. Wow!

My domicile was a quaint little hotel. Since it was not for tourists, there was no big reception desk, just a little room where the concierge could be found if anyone needed help. Further back, an older lady was manning the telephone.

I was shown to my room which was different from what I expected to find. Everything was in one big room. In one corner was a little kitchen with a small gas stove and a table. In the other corner was a king-sized bed and an armoire for my clothes. I did not stop to consider whether I liked or not. It was not important. All that mattered was that I was in the United States.

The next day I discovered that I could not start working until I got my United States licenses to practice my trade. Fortunately, with the one I had from Europe, I was able to get a reciprocal one here. That took about ten days and then, voila, I could work.

My first experience in a coiffure salon was somehow subdued. Nothing reminded me of Pierre Jacy's Waldorf Astoria Salon in New York or the ones in Mexico or anywhere else. I had to go down few steps in my perception of my trade in the United States. First, it was not a salon; it was shop, and for me it was very basic. The beauty shop in Evanston had five hairdressers. They were not hairstylists and I was not used to all that. Maybe my father was right. I might have to go back to salvage what I had left.

I was shown my station and introduced to my helper. The helper did the shampoos and provided me with whatever I needed to take care of my clients. Two of the hairdressers were middle-aged. Their work resembled what had been done in the 1930's and it was not very pretty. However, their customers wanted that type of work. Just for a moment I wondered what would happen when their customers died. I thought that those two hairdressers would no longer have jobs. For me, it was a humorous thought.

Next, there was a Frenchman who had lived in the United States for a long time. He was very negative about it. He was also not a very good hairstylist. He told me that he was going to write a book about how communism could save this country. I found that very odd and wondered why he stayed here. The fourth hairstylist, who really deserved that title, was from Holland. He was very good but did not seem to fit in terms of work with the others. I was the fifth hairstylist and I wondered what kind of trap I had jumped into.

That first day I had few customers, but they were very happy that a French hairstylist was taking care of them. Everyone liked my accent. I was the show for the day. At the end of the day I was satisfied. I had a good feeling, but I also had a lot of thinking to do.

On the way back to my hotel, I walked through a little park. It was summer and evenings were very nice. I sat on one of the benches and just looked around at nature. While I was sitting still, a squirrel came very close and sat across from me. He did not seem afraid and I did not move, but it was very funny because it seemed that he was waiting for me to start talking about my uncertainties. Back at the hotel, I just wanted to sleep and that's what I did. I even forgot to eat that night.

The next day when I went back to work, I decided to play it by ear for now and learn how things were done in my new country. For a few months, I just tried to get along with everybody and do a good job so my reputation would be enhanced.

I decided to socialize with my boss Georges. He was well known and owned many assets. I studied him in all aspects of doing business. After many nights of analyzing my situation, I decided that because of the way my trade is seen in this country, the best philosophy would be to create my own image by opening my own business. I was satisfied with my decision and decided not to look back.

Now that I had something to focus on, I decided that my boss would be the door to my aspirations. During the next year, I made a lot of acquaintances, some good, others not so good, but all were important. Georges had another beauty shop in Highland Park, north of Evanston. There I met a hairstylist from Switzerland whom I shall call Fritz. He and his wife became my best friends. I eventually became Godfather of their two children.

During that year, Fritz and the hairstylist from Holland and I became the most well-known hairstylists in George's beauty salon chain. We decided to work together and to promote ourselves through participation in hairstyle competitions. I was lucky enough to have the Illinois president of the hairstyling trade as a client. With her help, we were able to enter the different shows. I have to admit that we were very successful. Among the three of us, we always won. We also brought new techniques to hair cutting as well as to hair setting. Very quickly, we became so well known that we started to have new ideas.

During that time I also met a very nice couple whom I will call Mr. and Mrs. L. He was a very well-known personality in Chicago with a morning radio show at WBBM. Later on, Mrs. L. became a partner of mine in the Evanston beauty shop.

One day Georges told me that he was looking for a partner in the one-story building he owned where six businesses were paying rent. The Highland Park beauty salon was one of the businesses. After making some inquiries, I decided to go along. I needed to invest $2,000, which at the time I did not have. I had just purchased a 1960 Chevrolet Impala for $2,000 in cash.

I thought that the best way for me to get the money was to write to my father. But the answer from my father was direct: "Son, if you think that it is a good business and you present it well, the bank will lend you the money." Needless to say, I was very angry at him. However, after thinking about it for several days, I decided to follow his advice. I made my business plan and went to the Highland Park Bank. After my presentation to the president of that bank, the loan was approved. During the following years of doing business together, the president and I became good friends.

I felt as though I were in a boiling pot. I was doing things because they were there. I was making contacts with customers I thought could be of help in the future. I was also making acquaintances with other beauty shop owners. During that time, I made friends with three young hairstylists from Deerfield, close to Highland Park, who owned the Carriage Trade Beauty Salon. They were from Canada and lived in a very big, beautiful house with an old French gentleman whom later on I found was the financier. We became good friends and they encouraged me to buy my first house.

The old gentleman had no family and somehow he had unofficially adopted these three young artists. They were very talented, not only in their trade, but also in decorating their house. For a brief moment, it was nice to be among creative people again.

My first house was located in Lincolnshire, Illinois, a small community among tall trees. During the winter, I skated on the big pond and tried to play hockey with kids from the neighborhood. At that time I was a big hockey fan, but not a very good ice skater.

My first Christmas in the United States was spent with my friend from Switzerland and his family. We made it European style or, more accurately, Swiss style. We decorated the true pine tree and for the first time I was involved with putting electric lights on a Christmas tree. In Europe, we put real little candles that were lit for a short time during Christmas Eve and every night thereafter until the tree was ready to be used for fire wood.

After the holidays, I planned a trip to Florida in my new car. I had heard a lot about the state, good stories as well as some not-so-good ones. This was during the 1960's and segregation was still very much alive. However, for some reason I had never thought about segregation in real terms. The trip to Florida turned out to be an eye-opening journey.

A few unusual events happened along the way. While traveling through Georgia, I stopped at a chicken place. It was a wooden shack that looked as though it might collapse on itself at any moment. I even heard the cracking of the wooden steps. Inside, there were wooden tables and chairs that matched the shack. I could not say whether the floor was dirty or not, since it was black. My friend and I sat at a table and were told that this was the best place in the world for fried chicken. Fried chicken was another first for me. The only fried chicken I knew was the kind that my mother pan-fried at home. When the waitress brought the chicken, I had to fight my way through the heavy breading to get to the real thing. To this day, I don't care for fried chicken.

I had been in the United States for about seven months, so I thought that I could understand English well. I was wrong. There were two men sitting on the other side of the room talking to each other. While we were eating, I tried to catch some of their conversation. I could not believe that I did not understand a single word they were saying.

When we crossed into Florida, Route 1 was a two-lane highway. After a while, nature had to be taken care of. I stopped at a small rest area and was faced with my hardest test. The wooden rest rooms caught my eye. On the right side was a sign that said, "Whites only." On the left was a sign that said, "Negroes." I had a dilemma. My parents had raised me to never look down on anyone. Discrimination and segregation were things I knew about, but I had never had to deal with them before.

My thinking at the time went something like this. "If I go to the white-only side, I will be a hypocrite toward my beliefs. If I go to the Negro side, I will have a different problem. First, I am not a Negro. Second, I am white. Third, if someone sees me going to the wrong side, what could happen?" For the first time in my life, those questions were coming fast and furious. Eventually, I decided to retain the status quo. I went back to my car without taking care of my needs. Off and on, I continued thinking about this situation and was relieved that I did not have to handle this problem on a daily basis.

Florida was very nice. I was introduced to different foods. I went to *jai alai* matches that reminded me of Spain. However, I had to deal with the same segregation problem. I did not care for all the hotels on the beach, since it was hard for someone not staying in the hotels to get to the beach. All in all, Florida was a learning process and a successful trip for me.

Back in my house in Lincolnshire, my life was split between work for Georges and plans for the future. I felt like a little boy with a toy box. Since I had landed in my new country, I had been surrounded by so many opportunities that I felt everything was possible. I began thinking about buying a second car. I didn't need one, but it was the American way. So I bought a red Fiat sports convertible. It was a beautiful machine and it made me feel good. I also had to get a grip on the way anyone could buy things. Credit was new for me. To buy a house, I could understand credit, even though in Europe if the buyer did not have fifty percent in cash, there was no credit available.

At the beginning of my second year, the other two hairstylists and I were contemplating opening a new beauty salon in a northern suburb between Highland Park and Evanston. We needed first to sever our relation with Georges. That was a little tricky because both of them were under contract. However, a good lawyer resolved our problem to the satisfaction of both sides. I sold my shares of the building back to Georges and we were on our way.

Since credit was the way to do business, I also bought the salon in Highland Park and partnered with Mrs. L. in the Evanston salon. By then I had developed a very good business relationship with the Highland Park Bank and its president. At the time, I only had to call him and tell him what I was buying and the line of credit was mine. When I think of it now, it was a little scary.

After a few months, the new salon was very successful. The three of us had our following, so we only had to develop new customers for the other hairstylists we hired. After a year, we had seven stylists working in the store. Life was good for me, but it was never enough. Somehow, I felt that if I didn't plan the next thing, I was losing opportunities. I felt as though I were addicted to continuing to improve no matter what it was. During all that time, I worked very hard to develop a business relationship with the different beauty supply houses. Those relationships were very important for the development of new businesses, credit plans, and availability of information.

By the end of the second year, I decided to go back to France to visit my parents and friends. It was a trip that would show that I was doing well. It was also time to take care of the person in Paris whom I promised myself I would help. Before I could leave, I had to prove that I had paid my taxes, another law I was ignorant of.

The flight was uneventful until I arrived in Orly and decided to take a taxi into Paris. I was surprised to notice that everything was so small compared to the United States. The cars, the buildings, and even the streets were smaller. However, the streets had so much more personality that those in the United States.

In Paris I chose a small hotel at the Place Vendome which is close to everything, including the high couture boutiques. The hotel had an iron-work elevator with no roof that was very similar to the one in my father's office. My room was beautiful. The big window overlooked the Place Vendome and the streets made of cobblestones. The hotel was not far from my dad's office.

The trip was in many ways a disappointment for me. When I started to visit my friends, I realized that they were talking to me, but the friendship that we had before was no longer there. I felt as though they were jealous of me because I had left and they had stayed behind. I even tried to find Brest, who had been with me at École St. Augustin. His mother had always been worried about him. I thought that he would end up as a gangster. Maybe he did. I could not find him and his mother had not heard from him since we had left school. Hopefully he was not in jail somewhere.

Finally, I went to see Marcel, the man I had always tried to emulate. He no longer had his furniture-making business. Instead, he was working for a wood company as a salesman. When we met for dinner at the Montaigu's house, I expected everything to be just as it was before. The Montaigus received me like the André they had always known. They looked happy to see me and we had lots of things to talk about. It felt like home and the visit was heart-warming for me.

However, Marcel was not very talkative. Instead, he was just the opposite, quite disinterested. I did not say anything, but I was hurt. Back in my hotel after that dinner, I decided to end my friendship with all my old friends. My life was now in my new country. I realized that despite what I did not like in the United States, life there was better than here.

That settled forever the question of whether I would ever come back or not.

After taking care of my mission in Paris to help the beggar woman in the Place de Madelaine, the rest of the time was mine to enjoy. I had taken my parents for granted for a long time. Now we talked and shared stories about our lives. We went to movies, then to restaurants where we discussed our philosophies about the movies. We'd always enjoyed doing those things before and it felt good to spend time with them again.

We had a unique way of communicating that I expect that other multi-lingual families share. In our home, if people did not know at least three languages, they would not have been able to understand any conversations. Our family, as well as our extended family, used whatever language first came to mind. But the word roots and the endings of the words usually turned out to be in different languages.

We were so used to that form of communication that years later when Carolina and I were in New York, my cousin Tad Nowicki called and asked me what language I wanted to use. Even now, I sometimes start speaking in a different language to my wife before I catch myself doing that.

After visiting with my parents, I went to Les Halles de Paris. Les Halles was a huge marketplace where all businesses in Paris and the suburbs came for supplies. A person could find everything and everybody in that place. After the theater, movies, or even a hard day at work, people came for dinner, dancing, or a drink. One could rub elbows with movie stars, musicians, artists of all trades, as well as many beautiful women. Most of the cafés had small bands with accordion players so people could dance between the tables. Everyone said hello to everyone else, even those they didn't know. It had a fantastic ambiance. By seven o'clock in the morning, everyone was gone. Only the cleaning crew stayed behind.

I loved to eat clams and I knew that the best place to do that was at Les Halles. That night, I ate seven plates of clams. They were boiled in water with onion and spices and served plain. A few hours after I returned to my hotel, I had to call my dad because I did not feel good at all and I was in pain. When he came to my room with his doctor, I learned I had food poisoning. The doctor gave me a shot and when the day was over, I felt better. I was ready to continue enjoying Paris.

When people ask me about the best time to see Paris, I always say, "Four in the morning." Why four in the morning? "Well," I reply, "Paris is lit throughout the night and the traffic is at a minimum at 4 a.m. The store owners have cleaned the sidewalks in front of their shops and everything smells very nice. The main statues and monuments are all illuminated, but you are the only one there to see them. By 6:30 traffic starts to be a nuisance and the whole city starts to move again."

My trip to France was a mixture of questions and wonderings. I knew that I had moved forward with my life. Maybe it was not a perfect life, but I knew my future was somewhere ahead. As for my friends, either they had not grown or they had not progressed as quickly as I had. I could understand that because at the time France's way to do business was pompous. The opportunities were not as easy to grasp as those in the United States. But my trip had definitely helped me put one question to rest. Had I made a mistake going to the New World? The answer was "No." I knew I was really on my way to becoming an American.

Chapter 19

When I returned to the United States, I felt as though I were coming home. Now my thinking turned to "What's next?" rather than "What did I leave behind?" My life was mainly centered around the salons and my friendship with Fritz. My relationship with Fritz was good. I felt like part of his family.

The salons were doing good business. I owned the Evanston salon and was partnered with Georges in the Highland Park salon. Fritz and I owned the one in Glencoe. But the hairstylists were just average and that bothered me. I did not want to have an average business, since that was not what I was used to. However, at the time I was not sure what to do about it.

Being relatively new to the country, I was fascinated with the ease that I could acquire things. Through one of my customers, I was introduced to riding horses. I liked it very much and decided to pursue it seriously. After learning how to ride English, I invested in a young thoroughbred. With help from the stable trainer, I trained my own horse. He was a beautiful seventeen-hands-high jumper that I named The Flying Frenchman. Soon I started to enter him in hunting and jumping competitions.

Of course, I had to reorganize my working time. I decided to work in the mornings and spend the afternoons training and learning about horsemanship. My schooling was very interesting to me. I learned how to clean and maintain the saddle and the bridles, how to give the necessary shots, and how to groom my horse. I also learned how to shoe my horse, but I never had enough confidence to actually do it. If I were to make just a small mistake while shoeing, it could injure the animal for life. I was not ready to take that chance.

Every afternoon I trained with my horse in jumping and developing an understanding between the animal and myself. I felt like royalty. I never thought that I would have a trainer just for myself. I wanted to be good. Nothing was going to stop me. During the weekends, I rode as long as I could. During the winter, my schedule was the same. Actually, I enjoyed riding in the snow. We went as a group from the stable to ride in the forest all morning.

One day my trainer told me that my horse and I were ready for minor equestrian competition. I was ecstatic. In the next few months we had a great time learning the ins and outs of the trade. A few years later, we became proficient and entered equestrian competitions in Atlanta, New York, and Chicago. After these experiences, horsemanship became just a weekend pastime. During the few years that I was busy with horses, I also learned how to play polo and I purchased two polo ponies.

My pastime also gave me the opportunity to meet business people who could help me fulfill my business goals. While I was involved in the equestrian sport, I met a man named Richard Pick, who was a professional classical guitarist as well as an accomplished rider. He owned the Chicago School of Music and also wrote music for movies.

He and I became very good friends and I decided to again take lessons in classical guitar which I had stopped when I was living in Europe. It was time-consuming to work with Richard and to practice at home. My weekends were divided into little packets. I had only a certain amount of time to spend on each event. On Sunday afternoons Richard Pick and I gave small concerts for other students at his school. Between music and horses, Richard and I spent a lot of time together.

When I eventually became very proficient in playing classical guitar, I decided to jump into flamenco music which I had loved since I was a child. At the Chicago School of Music there was a Spanish teacher who wanted to make a small flamenco group. After some practice to take the rust out, he and I organized that group. No name, just good music.

One day after Richard and I finished practice, he indicated to me that I was good enough to go on tour with him. I listened with attention and I felt very proud of myself. However, I felt that I reached my goal. I had recognition from a master that I was good. In fact, I was even better than good since he was not afraid to do concerts with me. That was enough for me. From that day on, I did not practice seriously. I continued to play for myself and a few friends with no pressure. Richard and I stayed friends. From time to time we played together in private and we rode horses.

For me it was a beautiful time, but it was lost among so many other endeavors. During all that time, I realized that I could delegate responsibilities, rather than doing all the hairstyling myself. I could hire good hairstylists and become well known as long as they did excellent jobs under my name. This idea worked for me for some time, but I was not sure how to take advantage of it. One big obstacle was finding hairstylists who were aware of fashion trends in hair, clothing, designers, and accessories. However, for now I was so obsessed with my horsemanship that I dismissed the urgency of it.

Between working in the mornings and my equestrian duties, I learned another sport that I enjoyed, water skiing. Fritz had a boat and on summer afternoons, he and his two children and I went to Lake Forest to water ski. We had a rule that the first thing all of us did in the boat was to put on our safety vests. Another safety rule was that whoever was on the boat, but not piloting, would have the water skier in view at all times.

One day after we put the boat in the water, I decided that I would start from a wall embankment. As expected, I did very well. My skies hit the water and I stayed upright. I was a fairly good water skier and until that day, I had never fallen. Fritz was piloting the boat. His oldest son, who was about seven years old then, was supposed to watch me.

For no reason at all, I fell that day. At the time, I did not worry. However, I very quickly started to ponder my fate. I was once again facing the possibility of dying. When I was young, my mother and I had often feared death when the bombs fell around us in Poland. Now I wondered if I would die in a waterskiing accident in the United States.

The boat did not stop despite my yelling. Fritz's son was not looking when he should have been and there were a lot of fast boats in the vicinity. This was the only time I had not put on my vest because I had not gone into the boat first. The shore was about one mile away. I had never swum that far. I was not such a good swimmer anyway. I calmed myself down, but I was very worried that a fast boat would not see me and run over me. Only my head was above the water. After about ten minutes, a boat spotted me and threw me a life jacket. They did not even stop and I did not have chance to tell them that I was tiring. I put on the jacket and floated until Fritz came looking for me. It was an experience I never forgot. I found out that I could deal with dangers that directly involved me.

I will never forget another event. I remember very distinctly what I was doing and where I was. I was finishing a hair style for one of my clients when someone said, "The President has been shot!" Of course, that person was talking about President Kennedy. At first, I did not comprehend what was being said. I was in America. Something like that could not happen here. Then it hit me and every other person in the salon. We all listened to the radio for more news.

For the first time in my life, I felt as though I had lost a leader. I was puzzled by my feelings. I did not know the man and I did not have any political affiliation. Yet, at that moment, I felt an emptiness that I could not explain. For the next few days I was very careful about conversations with customers since I did not know how they would react. Most of the customers and people in the salon took the news even harder than I.

After John F. Kennedy's funeral, everything went back to normal. My partners and I were working hard in the Glencoe salon basement for the next hairstyle competition. This turned out to be the birth of new technology that would later be called "Pivot Point." It was on that technology that we built a school.

Meanwhile I was running between the salons trying to find ways to delegate work, rather than do it all myself. Since I had come to the United States, I felt like a small child with a toy box. Nothing seemed impossible. Within three years I was doing so well that I decided to do what many other Americans did --- get rid of my Chevrolet Impala and buy a Buick. It was winter in Chicago. Snow and ice in the suburbs covered all the roads. Road 22 was a narrow, two-way road that passed the entrance to Lincolnshire.

After I bought my new four-door Buick Electra 225, I decided to be very careful because of ice and snow on the road. So I took a longer detour on roads that were either wider or had very little traffic. However, at the end I was still left about half a mile from my house and I had to take Road 22 for that half mile. When I came to the stop sign before turning onto Road 22, I saw two cars coming. I decided to wait until they passed. However, the car behind the first one decided to pass it and then turn into the road where I was stopped. He started to slide towards me and I frantically tried to put my car into reverse, but to no avail. Needless to say, my car stopped his slide. I was not hurt but the left side of my Buick was twisted metal. I remember that I started to laugh, seeing humor in what had happened. I had a new car that had not yet seen my garage and already it had to be repaired.

I had spent Christmas with my friend Fritz and his family. For New Year's we decided to go to Wisconsin to snowmobile. At the time I still was very susceptible to popping noises. It was a residue of the bombing when I was a little boy in Poland during the war. Current research about Post Traumatic Stress Disorder suggests that exposure therapy can help people overcome the debilitating effects. People are gradually exposed to sights and sounds that simulate their trauma to help them learn to cope. I had spent much of my life struggling to deal with one symptom after another. But that night, I was unprepared for what happened.

When it was close to midnight, Fritz, his wife, and a friend and I decided to stop at a bar to celebrate the New Year. We sat at a table and ordered our champagne. When midnight came and the noise-makers were popping, I jumped every time I heard a pop. Some people noticed my reaction to the noise and started to go around our table popping the little bottles that sprayed confetti. The more I jumped, the more people came and popped the noise-makers. It became so bad that I had to leave and go outside to calm down. Now, many years later, I can look back on this experience and be thankful that I no longer suffer from any of my previous symptoms.

The next day I felt much better. Our New Year's lunch buffet was something I had never seen. The buffet table seemed a mile long. The ice sculptures reached all the way to the ceiling. Afterwards, we went snowmobiling, another first for me. It was hard on my back, but the fun was much more important. We spent two days on the machines. When we were ready to go back home, we could hardly walk, but we were happy and satisfied.

After New Year's, the days seemed pretty mundane. I had to make sure that the customers were happy. The hairstyling trade is a cut-throat business, so I needed to make sure that we were at the top in terms of service. I also had to find a way to bring hairstylists from Europe.

On the more pleasant side, my parents decided to visit me. Coming to the United States on the ocean liner *S.S. France* was a first for them. The *S.S. France* was the most modern ship crossing the Atlantic at that time. My parents landed in New York at the beginning of summer. We stayed in New York for a few days, then drove to Chicago. I was happy that my parents had come to visit. I wanted to know if my dad approved my move to the United States. After he saw New York and the country-side, I thought he might be as impressed as I had been. However, as usual he was very reserved and I never asked the question.

In Chicago, the three of us shopped for a car. My father wanted to buy a Corvair, the first rear-engine car made by General Motors. As far as I was concerned, it was a cheap car and not the standard that he was used to. However, that is what he wanted and he said it was for a good reason. He wanted a small car for Paris traffic and had decided it had to be an American car. The one he liked was dark red outside with black leather inside. The whole package had my mom's blessing, so everybody was happy.

Back in Lincolnshire the next day, my father wanted to take his new car for a ride. I explained the differences in driving habits here and in France so that he could make a better decision as to whether he wanted to drive here or not. He said he had no problems and so we went. We were on a quiet road with no traffic and my dad was doing well. In the distance was a road on the right that merged with ours. When my dad was near the merging road, he saw a car on the right. In Europe, the car coming from the right has the right of way, so my dad slammed on the brakes. He forgot that the car on the right had to yield. The tires smoked and squeaked. The car behind us didn't expect our sudden stop and crashed onto the rear of my dad's new car. The car had to be towed. No one was hurt, but my dad was unable to take the car with him on the ship. After it was repaired, I shipped it to him.

One day my mom and I started to talk. She was in pain, but I did not know why. She was sitting on the couch, relaxed, I thought. Then she told me in a very calm voice, "André, I have breast cancer and that is what is giving me pain." She continued, "I am taking homeopathic medication. I think it will work for me." After some more discussion about her condition, she said, "You know I don't want to die, but if I have to and it happens, there is nothing I can do about it." At the time I did not know what to say and I continued the conversation as though what she had said was just a normal discussion.

During the rest of my parents' stay, the cancer question was not revisited. She was very confident that the medication she was taking was going to work. Later on I realized how strong mentally she must have been to accept the inevitable. In my mind I went over every word she had said. Each time I went over the words, they took on greater importance.

I wanted my mother to experience a real American pastime, so I took her to Lake Zurich, outside Chicago, where Fritz and I water skied. On the way there was a little restaurant where I always stopped. It had the best hamburgers I had ever eaten and I don't even like hamburgers.

However, these were served with onions on Kaiser rolls. Afterwards, we walked by the lake, sat on a bench, and talked about my life in the United States. It was the first time since we had been in Sweden that we shared such togetherness. It felt good to be together. It was a little bit of home.

When it was time for my parents to go back to France, we drove to New York where they boarded the ship. Later my dad told me that when they arrived and were going through immigration, my mother was exhibiting bizarre behavior. So she was escorted to a room where the authorities interrogated her about bringing in and being on drugs. However, they soon found out that she was only half-conscious because of the pain. A few weeks later, I was told that she had been admitted to a private clinic, but nothing else was said.

One month later I received a phone call from my dad saying that my mother was dead. That same day I booked my flight to Paris. When I arrived, I went straight to Vigneux where my mother was. At home my father asked me if I wanted to see my mother. At first I said no because I wanted to remember her as I had always known her. After a while, however, I changed my mind and I saw her. She was in a wooden coffin on dry ice. At that time in France, dead people were not embalmed, so she was on dry ice to give me time to come from the United States. She was very thin and pale. I could not believe that she was the same person I had been with at Lake Zurich.

After I saw my mother, her coffin was put in the middle of our salon. She stayed there overnight and the funeral was scheduled for the next day. My father stayed by the coffin through the night and in the morning before the hearse arrived, I saw my dad crying. I did not say anything to him. I felt that it was his time and he should not be disturbed. I knew that the tomb she would be placed in would be well taken care of because the cemetery belonged to the Boucher family. Their son, who was in our Three Musketeers group when we were young boys, was now in charge of the family business.

This was the first time that I participated in a funeral. The only funerals I had seen were in the cowboy movies I'd watched when I was a child. Oddly enough, my mother's funeral reminded me of those classic black-and-white films. The hearse was a black wagon with a flat, black roof from which black trimmings were hung. The hearse was pulled by four beautiful black horses. The family and friends walked behind the hearse. Maybe it is strange to say, but I enjoyed her funeral. It was different and much more down-to-earth than I'd expected. After the funeral

I did not feel sad. Actually, I was convinced that this is how my mom would have liked it if she had had her say.

Later I found a picture of my mother watering flowers in her hospital room the same afternoon she died. Maybe this is why I did not feel sad. One moment she was watering flowers and the next she was gone. It seems as she did not suffer then, but this is just a thought. Years later, I am still happy that I decided to see her in the coffin.

Another thing that I discovered about myself is that I am not sad at funerals. For some reason, I always see something positive in every situation. The way I see it, when my mother was dead, she did not have any feelings. Only the survivors have feelings about the one who left. So I don't see any reason for me to be sad.

After few more days with my dad to make sure he was doing well, I had to return home. I did not feel sad, but I did feel more resolute about pursuing my endeavors in the United States.

Chapter 20

My partners and I decided that we were ready to open the Pivot Point School. The name Pivot Point came from the geometric form that we designed. The technique we invented became the foundation for our hairstyles and hair cuts. Instead of using ordinary rollers in traditional straight lines, we developed a method of setting hair with tapered rollers in spiral formations. This created a more natural style that held longer.

To prepare for the school, we decided to divest ourselves of the Glencoe Salon. That was not difficult. The hard part was forgoing liver and onions. There is a story behind this. A few months after we opened the salon, a lady opened a very small restaurant a few doors from our business. There were just a few tables; most of the orders were to go. On Wednesdays, however, customers lined up almost around the building because the lady served liver and onions that were out of this world. It was the first time that I had tasted liver and onions prepared that way. At home we had chicken livers, but nothing like what this lady could fix. In our minds the liver and onions were the biggest loss in leaving Glencoe.

We had to find a building with a good location and close by transportation for our school. It took us a few months, but we found exactly what we wanted. We could have the entire second floor of a large building that had good parking and access to transportation. The building was in Chicago very close to Evanston. Actually, one side of the street was Chicago and the other was Evanston. Within three weeks the school was opened and we did not have much problem getting students since we were pretty well-known by then.

But for me, after the school opened, something was missing. I was not happy with my partners. I also discovered that teaching was not my thing. So after a few months, I decided to sell my shares to the school and to continue on my own.

I also was in the process of selling my shares of the building I owned with Georges in Highland Park. I found out that Georges was not a very honest person and when I confronted him, he answered, "There is a sucker born every day." Now I had just one store in Evanston.

My idea to have something on the Gold Coast on the north of Michigan Avenue could finally become a reality. Through a friend, I met a German hairstylist I will call Kurt. He was interested in opening a salon, but he was not sure about doing it by himself. After few months, I met the owner of the Carriage House which was located on Michigan Avenue and Chicago Avenue. He was interested in having a high-style salon for the upper-class customers who patronized his establishment.

Before proceeding any further, I had to find a lawyer. That was not too difficult since one of my customers was the wife of one. She organized a meeting between her husband and me. After I met with him for several hours to lay out my plans for the future, he agreed to become my lawyer on a retainer. Now my next move was to agree on principles with my new partner.

The most important work in front of us was designing a salon that was both practical and pleasant for customers. We also had to develop an advertising plan so potential customers would know where we were. The financing for the salon was not difficult. Because of my good business history, I had only to call the Highland Park Bank and present my friend, the president, with a good business plan. The challenge was to work with suppliers and the architect for the layout and furniture, as well as for future supplies. The program was very exciting. I was going to have a salon in the most affluent part of Chicago. I considered selling the Lincolnshire house, since I was living too far away.

By now, it was 1965, a memorable year for me. A lot of things happened to change my life's direction. Since I had been in the United States for five years, I was eligible to become a citizen. I knew I needed a lawyer who could help me through the paper maze. Through my business lawyer, I met Albert, who had worked for the immigration department for fifteen years. Now he was the top Chicago union lawyer. Besides helping with my naturalization papers, he agreed to help me import hairstylists from Europe.

I received a thick, heavy book with major American information, including the political system and how it works. I spent several months studying and had friends quiz me for hours on end until I was sure that I was ready. I thought that to become citizens of this great country, people had to be knowledgeable about its history and political system so they could vote and make sensible decisions about important matters.

Finally, my test day arrived and I was ready. I was glad that Albert was with me. For the first time, I felt overwhelmed. I was out of my comfort zone and I did not know exactly how to handle the bureaucrats. After signing a multitude of papers under Albert's watchful eye, I was asked to follow a lady to her office. The office was like a cubicle with glass on top of a wooden wall. She sat behind her desk and started to talk to me very slowly, as though I could not understand her. I did not want to hurt her feelings, so I did not say anything. I just let her think that I was what she expected.

The first test was a written one. She said a sentence and told me to write it. She said, "Please write, 'She will buy some milk.'" I was a little perplexed and waited for more. To my astonishment, she asked for what I had written. Then she handed me a piece of paper from which she asked me to read, "John is going to work on a bicycle." She took the paper back and did not say anything.

Next, she said, "I will now ask you a few questions." She asked me who the two senators from Illinois were. At that time I knew only one, Senator Dirksen, a Republican. The other was a Democrat whose name escaped me. So I swiftly said, "I am a Republican." She smiled and told me that the test was over. She indicated that I passed and that in due time I would receive the date that I would be sworn in to become an American.

I was happy that my naturalization test was behind me, but I was also very disappointed because I had studied hard and she had asked me such simple questions. Looking at it now, I probably wanted to show how much I knew, but I never had the chance. When I left the immigration office, Albert was smiling. I never asked him what was so funny, but he probably knew what was going to happen before I went for my test.

The name of the new salon was AlexAndré. The Alex came from my professional European name and André came from my real name. The idea was to come as close as possible to the AlexAndré name, since he was the most well-known hairstylist in the world, without infringing on any proprietary laws. AlexAndré was a very nice place with chandeliers and a lot of mirrors so the place looked larger that it was. The hairstylists' stations were wood trimmed in gold. We had a perfume and make-up bar, as well as a massage room.

For the Grand Opening, we had a party for the affluent people living in or around the Gold Coast. It was a success. I noticed that most of the customers were going to be Jewish. I knew that Jewish customers tended to know one another and belonged to the same clubs. Most of the time, one person had a big influence on much of the group. If I pleased that person, I would probably get everyone else. However, if I displeased the leader, I risked losing most of that particular group.

Before our first day of business, I reminded the entire staff about the importance of first-class service by telling them about what I once witnessed. One evening when I had a salon in Highland Park, I walked toward the Cadillac dealership. I went in and looked at the cars. They were very nice, but I was just passing time since I didn't want to buy one. A man with dirty boots and a very sad-looking hat came in. Since it was the beginning of winter, he was wearing a very raggedy coat.

I knew the man, so I said hello. He continued to look at the Cadillacs. No one else greeted the man. The two young sales people stayed in their office. After about ten minutes, the man motioned to a third person who had just come in from the back and he said to her, "Please, I will take this one and this one." as he pointed to the cars he wanted. When it was time for him to pay, he put his rough hand into his pants pocket and retrieved a roll of money and paid cash. The man was one of the biggest builders in the area. I indicated to my people to be very careful and not to judge our customers by how they looked. I told them that service must be first class all the time.

While the business at the new salon was growing, my partner and I decided to buy the same model car. I wanted a Jaguar XKE, a stylish sports car. Actually, it was an *avant garde* style with a very long nose that made it very aerodynamic. The two of us went to the Imperial Motor Co. in Wilmette, on the north shore of Chicago. We chose the same model car, the same color, and the same style. However, we discovered that we had to wait six months before the cars could be delivered.

I was excited to be able to afford such a car. During the six-month wait, I mentally traveled everywhere I knew in the new car. I envisioned loading and unloading luggage many times. The anticipation of driving the real car was very exciting and adrenaline was running strong.

Finally, I received a call from the dealer that our cars were ready. I called my partner. We could hardly wait to sit behind the wheel. When we arrived, we rushed to see our new purchases. But I could not understand what happened next. For no reason at all, my excitement vanished. I was almost disappointed, but I did not know why. Then it hit me. My Jaguar ended up being just a car with four wheels. It was still a nice car, but nothing like I was expecting. Looking at the moment now, I realize that the months of anticipation could not live up to the reality.

Later on, when I thought about it, I decided to take the lesson from that experience and put it into practice in my life. At first, I was not exactly sure what was in that lesson, but I decided to be careful in any future business decisions and to be humble and not try to show off. I felt uncomfortable when people made nice comments about my car. But at the same time I knew I was fitting into the milieu of my customers.

Even though I had mixed feelings about having the car, I wanted to go on a long trip like the ones I'd imagined while waiting for the Jag. A friend and I decided to go to Colorado, where I had an acquaintance close to Colorado Springs. The inside of the car was beautiful. I loved the stick shift. It made me feel in control of a racing car. The purr of the engine was sexy. Loading the car with suitcases was a highlight of the trip, just as I had dreamed while waiting.

I wanted to open up the car somewhere on a straight road to see how it would behave. I'd never been to Kansas, but it seemed like the place to do it. The roads were straight and flat, there was no traffic, and I could see for many miles. The road was a two-lane road, but it was very nice with no bumps or potholes.

By the time I made the decision to open up, I did not realize that I was going 90 miles an hour. I continued to accelerate and the speedometer climbed to 110...120...130... The speedometer dial rose to 160, but I when reached the speed of 148 miles an hour, to my astonishment, the inside of the car it felt like an airplane. At the end of the road was a slight turn. When I slowed down, the speedometer showed 90 miles an hour, but it felt like I was doing 30. Needless to say, I was impressed. However, I was not a speed demon and I never reached such high speeds again.

In Colorado, my car did not perform as well because of the altitude. When I was in the mountains, the engine was sluggish. It was a bizarre feeling to push the accelerator and not have the car respond.

We arrived at my friend's dude ranch with a lot of expectations on my part. It was early spring and the ranch had to prepare for future customers. The ranch was in a valley surrounded by mountains. It had beautiful quarters for the clients, including a swimming pool and all the comforts. On the other side were accommodations for the ranch hands, stables, hayride wagons and barns. Very few horses were at the ranch then, just the ones used by the cowboys. The ranch had over two hundred horses grazing in the mountains. Now it was time to bring them down and get them ready for the tourist season.

The best part was that I would be a cowboy for a week. I wore boots, hat, and chaps, and was ready to ride in the mountain with the ranch hands. I was going to live the life I had seen in the cowboy movies when I was growing up in France. I had to make a few changes in my riding style. Western riding is different. The saddle is bigger and has a horn in front to tie the lasso. The horse does not need as much direction. Control of the horse is done by reins and changing position of the rider's weight.

We were ten: nine cowboys and one wannabe. It was just like in the movies. The chuck wagon was very similar to the ones I'd seen in the movies, except for the rubber wheels and no roof. It was pulled by two horses and had all the cooking necessities. Everybody had his own pack attached to the back of the saddle. The pack consisted of rain gear, tin utensils, and a sleeping bag. There were no tents. We were going to sleep under the sky. For me it was very exciting. I had never been in that environment.

It took us all day to reach our destination. Now the fun was going to start. The cook prepared the rolling kitchen by starting a fire. Then he actually hung a big pot over the fire. He also put a tin coffee maker on the fire, just like in the movies. I stood there with my jaw hanging open. It was a fabulous time for me. When it was time to eat, we all sat on the ground, legs crossed, and ate a delicious dinner.

After a while, everybody went to sleep. Except that I could not. I still could not believe what was happening. I was sure I was in a movie, sleeping in a sleeping bag with the stars for a roof. I felt quiet and noisy at the same time. I could hear all types of noise that I could not identify. The night was very clear. It made me feel that by extending my hand, I could touch the stars.

The next morning we mounted the horses and went to work. The leader made five teams of two and we went looking for the horses. Our job was to bring the horses into a fenced clearing. From there, we had to take them to the dude ranch. To find all the horses took us three days, plus another two days to guide them to the ranch.

The ranch was also known for setting up rodeos to find out which bulls and horses could perform well at a higher level rodeo. To that end, the ranch had two or three rodeos per week during the tourist season. Because I was young and I thought I was indestructible, I decided to compete in one of the rodeos. That is how I was introduced to barrel racing. The barrels were placed in a triangle. I do not remember the distance between the barrels, but it was long enough for the horse to gallop and slalom between them. It took a lot of talent to know how to control the horse and make him turn on his hind legs while galloping. I have to admit that after practicing for a day, I was able to compete without embarrassing myself.

The next step was to try to ride a bull. To this day, I don't know what possessed me to even think about riding a bull. I know that I was coaxed into doing it, but it was still my decision. I have to say that no amount of training would have helped. It was not very pretty. After I was told what to do, the cowboys helped me sit on the bull in a very tight pen so he could not move. When the bull was released, the only thought I had was how to jump off. The second I stayed on the bull seemed to be an eternity. Then, boom! I found myself on the ground, lucky not to have been trampled. The fall made me realize that I had no business riding a bull or putting myself in dangerous situations. But I had had my cowboy time and it was tremendous.

After two weeks, it was time to go back and continue to build my business. After the Carriage House with the AlexAndré salon, I had an eye on another salon in Glencoe. However, I still had to develop the salon on the Gold Coast where the affluent customers were asking for me. The more I thought about it, the faster I wanted to be back.

In Chicago, I had many things on my mind. I wanted to get rid of the salon in Evanston, to build up AlexAndré, and to get the salon in Glencoe. I also needed to organize my new living quarters at the Hollywood Towers. I had a one-bedroom apartment that needed an interior decorator. I loved my situation, but I had lots to do and very little time to do it. I was discovering that I worked very well under pressure, a trait that would continue to benefit me over the years.

Chapter 21

Colorado was nice, but now work was the main subject. While I was in Colorado, my German partner had kept AlexAndré afloat. I mean exactly what I said: he had just barely kept it afloat. I found out that I probably would be much better doing everything by myself instead of having a partner. He turned out to be an expensive cleaning man.

However, before I attempted to remedy that situation, I wanted to finish my apartment. I always liked to have a clean and organized place to come to after work so I could relax. Chicago Merchandise Mart near the Chicago River had very nice furniture and interior decorator facilities. After spending few days with the decorator, my apartment was going to have a complete face lift. The interior decorator came up with sketches of how it would look. I must say that it was looking very good. The main color scheme was medium blue. I told the decorator to follow the ideas in the drawings, except for my music corner. There, I wanted some specific items by the window from which I could see Lake Michigan.

In my music corner, I had a wooden high chair with a place to put my left foot at a medium height so that the body of the guitar rested comfortably on my thigh. For my right foot, I had a special wooden footrest set lower to keep a good balance. I also had a light wooden guitar holder and a matching music holder. When my apartment was finished, it looked beautiful and very comfortable. When I sat in my music corner looking at the water and playing, I felt both relaxed and artistic.

My apartment was situated on the twentieth floor. The building had its own food store on the first floor. It also had two swimming pools. Even better, I was living only a short drive from the Gold Coast. I had a reserved parking space for my Jag at the apartment, as well as at the Carriage House, which was great during winter time.

One year, a late blizzard hit Chicago, which was most unusual because winter was almost over. That morning when I looked from my apartment down to the street, it did not seem like much snow. However, when I went outside, there was hardly any traffic because everybody was stuck in the snow. I decided to get something for breakfast from the building's food store. To my amazement, there was hardly anything left in the store. People from the building had ransacked the store. How long do these people expect the storm to last, I wondered. It was inconceivable to me that anyone could be so selfish. So much for my breakfast! After spending much of the day at the salon, my return to the apartment took over four hours, instead of ten minutes on a normal day.

I had accomplished one thing: my apartment was livable. Now a more difficult task was in front of me. I needed to dispose of my German partner. Buying out my partner made my dad very happy. When my dad came to visit me for about two months and learned that my partner was a German, he was not at all happy. It was very understandable since he was Jewish and half of our family had died in concentration camps. I tried to talk to my dad and convince him that not all Germans were bad, but he did not want to hear this nonsense. However, when he was in my partner's presence, my father was always a gentleman.

During my father's visit, he spent time every day at the salon close to the cashier. He never told me if he was happy. He never said anything else about my business. Obviously, I was successful at the time, but not in the intellectual way he had hoped. After awhile, I became too busy and I never thought about it anymore.

Buying out a partner who does not want to be bought out is not an easy task. I do not remember the specifics of our contract, but I knew I could do it with the help of my lawyer. It was hard for me because there was nothing personal. He was a good person, but not a good business man. It was hard on my psyche every time I worked with him while the lawyers were battling it out. Three months later, I was the sole owner and ready to build the business my way.

Now that I was in the right environment on the Gold Coast, I needed the best hairstylists money could buy. Albert, my immigration lawyer, drew up the contracts for the European hairstylists. Within three months, I had two hairstylists from across the Atlantic, one from England and one from France. In a very short time, the salon was humming full speed.

The service started when a valet parked their cars for free. I also added a high-fashion apparel corner. The customers were served breakfast, lunch, or dinner while being cared for. Because of the high quality service and merchandise, people started to come from all parts of Chicago. The salon must have been well advertised by word of mouth because we had a lot of out-of-state clientele who made appointments months in advance of their Chicago arrival.

My two best-known clients were Ginger Rogers and Grace Bumbry. Ginger Rogers was a fabulous customer. She was very nice, grateful to receive good service, and absolutely unpretentious. She was a wonderful person and we were honored to care for her.

I saw Ms. Bumbry, a mezzo-soprano, in several operatic roles, including *Carmen*. Like Ms. Rogers, she was a very graceful and fantastic lady. It was nice to be involved with entertainment stars even if it was just for a short time. They were often on tour and came to my salon while they were in Chicago.

While at the Carriage House, I developed good, personal communications with everybody. The hotel manager, who was Greek, became a friend of mine, and so did most of the hotel workers. The salon provided the Three Hussars Restaurant with a lot of business and its owner and I became good friends.

The owner of the restaurant was a *bon vivant* who approached me and wanted to know if I liked to play poker. I said, "Yes, of course." He then proceeded to organize a poker game every Wednesday. The first Wednesday, I did not know what to expect. To my surprise, affluent people participated. Needless to say, to be in this weekly poker game, one needed to have some change. The pot was sometimes up to several thousand dollars. The game lasted all night with the food being provided by the Three Hussars. The Carriage House provided the room and the front desk. For their service, they received a generous tip.

AlexAndré Coiffure was doing well. It was a lot of work, but I was happy and very busy. Eventually, I decided to slow down for a while and enjoy both my work and Chicago. Besides my work at AlexAndré, I enjoyed going out with friends. I even reconnected with a friend from the other side of the Atlantic. At the time, Chicago was building a professional soccer team. To do that and be competitive, the Chicago coach imported players from foreign countries, including France.

One day while reading the sports pages of the Chicago newspaper, I recognized a name I knew when I was playing in France. He was Marcel

Novak, a professional soccer player with the Monaco team. I played with him and against him, so it was nice to see him again. After being in Chicago a short time, he was not happy with the team and he wanted out from under his contract. Since he was new in this country and did not have a lawyer, I suggested that he use my lawyer. After a short time, he and his family went back to France. It was his gain and my loss.

While I was enjoying myself and taking time to look around, I had two funny experiences. One day before I parked my Jaguar in the underground parking, I bought some French cheese. I am partial to French cheese and wine. The cheese that I liked best, Portsalut, has a very strong smell when it's well-aged. I liked this cheese to be aged since that is when the flavor is at its best. When the driver brought my car, I heard the tires squealing at each turn. Then the car arrived at great speed and the driver jumped out and handed me the keys without waiting for his tip. When I got into the car, I started to laugh. The whole car smelled like aged cheese. I am sure the driver thought it was something else!

The other experience happened early in the morning at the corner of Michigan and Chicago Avenues. The Armory was in the middle block on Chicago Avenue and at the time the circus was performing daily. I was standing on the corner when six elephants turned the corner into Chicago Avenue. At that moment a man with a briefcase tried to rush across the street at the corner. He stopped and, with a bewildered look, said in a loud voice, "I did not have a drink yet, but I see elephants!" He said it loud enough that people standing on the corner all started to laugh.

Enjoying myself did not stop me from looking at opportunities. After few years in the United States, my views about the hair styling business were changing from totally artistic to a compromise of less artistic and more money. It seemed to me that a great number of business people I talked to did not care much about quality or the artistic point of view. As long as the business could be sold, it was good enough for them. That philosophy was completely new for me and I decided to put it to work.

Not far from the Hollywood Towers where I was living was a salon that was hard to see from the Sheridan Road. I wondered why this beauty salon was doing fantastic business. After a little investigation on my part, I discovered that the salon was located in a middle-income Jewish neighborhood, the clientele was middle aged, and the salon's prices were very reasonable. As far as I was concerned, it was a good investment, not only in terms of money, but also since the work was not high-fashion quality, I would not have to import any stylists. After few months, I was the new owner of the salon. I did not change the name or the hairdressers because I didn't want to disturb anything that might slow down the business. I really didn't have much to do. The salon had a very capable lady who managed everything.

By now I had a CPA who took care of all the financial business for me. He was a friend of my business lawyer, so I had a good mini-board of directors. While discussing the immediate future with my small board of directors, the idea of having my own hair product came to mind. It was a good program, but I was not yet ready for it. The second idea was to franchise my beauty salons. I was not ready for this because when I don't understand a program completely, I shy away from it until the time comes when I can make sense of it. In retrospect, not following their recommendations was my biggest mistake.

I was interested in a salon located in Glencoe. It was owned by an Olympic ice skating champion who had won a gold medal. It was a very nice salon with a good upper-class clientele. Glencoe was an affluent North Chicago suburb, primarily Jewish, and well-situated in relation to downtown Chicago. It is on the way to Wisconsin and Lake Zurich and other very well-to-do towns. As far as I was concerned, it was a good investment and presented the possibility of having a second salon involved with high styling. Now the question was, "Does the owner want to sell?" My lawyer, who was experienced in that line of business, was the main negotiator.

I had enough on my plate for now and I wanted to take some time to enjoy myself. I became a hockey fan. From time to time, I went to see basketball games when friends provided the tickets. It was really by chance that most of my friends and acquaintances were in the restaurant business. That was very helpful when I wanted to go out. I hardly ever waited for a table, whether it was at Maxim's in the Drake Hotel or the famous French restaurant, *La Petite Chemineé*. There were other places, but I have forgotten their names.

At the time, I hired a young woman as personal business consultant. She prepared a program to appear on radio shows, television spots, as well as to the affluent Chicago crowd. To make the program work, she and I had to go to certain parties and restaurants where I could be seen and presented to potential future clients. The program was quite successful and the AlexAndré salon benefited from it. I cannot say the work was unpleasant. To the contrary, it was an eye-opener. The food was good. So was the entertainment.

But I did not feel in control of what was happening. Things were going so fast that at times I forgot the direction I wanted to go. The idea of high styling was getting blurred with the idea of the money that could be made. I felt that my values were being eroded for something that I did not know exactly how to handle. However, I did not see any big or dangerous effects from this change, so I did not do anything to stop it. In fact, it was rather pleasant to feel that people were interested in me. It was almost like being in Paris. So for some time, I did not worry much about things. Life was good.

Chapter 22

MR. ANDRÉ SALON

After relaxing for some time and enjoying meeting other business people, it was time to concentrate on acquiring the salon in Glencoe. It was a well-known salon because its name was that of a famous gold-medal-winning ice skater. The salon catered to an affluent clientele. Because the salon had a very good reputation and I could not compete with the name, even though my professional name was known, I had to prepare a program that would retain those good customers. For that, I had to give a better service and deliver a better product.

At the same time, I did not want to travel from Chicago to Glencoe every day, so I had to find a place near the salon. I was lucky because I knew the son of the largest real-estate broker on the North Shore. I contacted him to find something appropriate. I found out that he owned a two-story house in Ravinia, a very nice area near Ravinia Park, where the Chicago Symphony performed during the spring, summer, and fall.

I rented the second floor of that house. The place was beautiful and quiet and only a short drive from the Glencoe salon. My friend, who lived on the first floor, was a young man like me, so we got along well. Through him, I became acquainted with marijuana. I personally never touched the stuff, but he showed me his hiding place just I case I wanted to try. For a moment I wondered if staying there was a good idea. However, I decided that was his business and I had nothing to do with it.

The salon took half a block and had good parking on the street. The building was made of white brick with display windows. Inside there was room for make-up, hair coloring, and massage. There was also a large waiting room from which the customers could see the retail display.

The receptionist had a large, oval desk made of white brick. The large shampoo area was all in black. The salon's colors were blue and black, along with the wall of white brick.

When I became interested in the salon, the services were very basic. However, I planned to upgrade to include massage, make-up, lunch for the hungry customers, and whatever else the clientele wanted. At the beginning, I would do the make-up service, as well as hairstyling. Later, a professional make-up artist trained the most talented hairstylists.

When the employees were told that a new owner might come, the response was very positive. I made a special effort to meet all the employees before the sale was completed. Through the meetings, I found out that a few of the hairstylists planned to leave. They told me that they had a strong attachment to the previous owner. I could understand their situation because she was charismatic and good to her employees.

To build the salon as a high-level hairstyling entity, I needed to import three first-class hairstylists. My contacts in England worked with me to find hairstylists who had wanted to come to the United States for a long time. But they also needed to have high standards and be technically strong.

In general, it took three months to arrange for a hairstylist come to work in the USA. I contacted my immigration lawyer to set into motion importing the hairstylists from England. I was working within a very limited window. I wanted to time the buying of the salon with the arrival of the new hairstylists.

The difference between hairdressers and hairstylists is significant. Hairdressers are told by a client what to do because she thinks she knows what is becoming to her. In contrast, a hairstylist suggests what would be becoming to that particular customer. It is a big difference. Hairstylists must be very knowledgeable about the physical differences of each person. They must be very secure in themselves. Communication is paramount and the presentation of a new idea must be done carefully and positively.

A few months after I bought the salon, as stipulated in the contract, I changed the name to Mr. André Salon. For the next month, I built an advertising plan designed to keep as many customers as possible, and, of course, to develop new ones. A month after I bought the salon, I had assembled a very good team that could provide the customers with the best of everything. I was proud of the shampoo department. The three young ladies doing shampoos were very knowledgeable in hair care and were able to suggest remedies for any customer's problems.

The hairdressing department was wonderful since it could adapt to any circumstances in terms of hair color, hair cut, and hair style. The make-up department consisted of two people: myself and a make-up artist who worked on Fridays and Saturdays. The salon also had three manicurists who provided their service while the customers were under the hairdryers. All in all, I was very satisfied with the team I had assembled.

After a few months of new ownership, the salon was humming full speed. The affluent clientele was very nice. The word had spread that we were very good and that helped bring customers from other states. There was a good and honest relationship between all the hairstylists and the clientele. Everything seemed to fit together: the quality of services was excellent, the team had class, and the customers were satisfied.

I think that one of the reasons for the clientele confidence in us was the professionalism shown by everybody when a customer confided in one of us. There is a side to this profession that is very important to understand. After a customer becomes a regular with a hairstylist, she will often confide very personal information to that hairstylist. It was not any different in Mr. André Salon. There seemed to be a popular boredom in the married life of most affluent women who came to the salon. The most common complaint was that their husbands were hardly ever home. When they were home, quality time was not apparent. Because of these phenomena, it was very important that the chosen hairstylists not only be good at the trade, but also have very strong morals.

I personally had very nice customers. One of them who lived in Lake Forest was the wife of the Atlanta Braves baseball team owner. She always had nice things to say to me. I liked to style her hair because she trusted me to do what was most becoming to her. She came several times a week. Her personality was such that when she came to the salon, the atmosphere brightened.

I was also honored to have a customer from Wisconsin who was the owner of a large ice cream company. She was in the process of selling that business to a big conglomerate. She and her husband also owned a restaurant on the second floor of a hotel located on the Gold Coast on the north side of Michigan Avenue close to the Water Tower. After some time, she asked me if I would be interested in getting involved in her restaurant business. She wanted me to manage it for her, but I was enjoying my salon too much to want to take on this new challenge.

Since an affluent group of people frequented the salon, over the course of several years, everything seemed possible. I felt confident that if I chose to say yes, I would be unstoppable. I did not see the potential dangers until much later. My customers and their husbands sometimes offered me both legal and illegal business opportunities that were very hard to refuse. Some of those offers went as far as the top people in state government.

At that time I was living in Ravinia, a very up-scale part of Highland Park. Since I was in this milieu, I could not see that I was becoming part of it. My interest in women was superficial, more physical than anything else. I felt strongly that most of the women I was in contact with through my trade were very shallow. They seemed to want to put some excitement into their boredom. Personally, I was not interested in anything serious as far as a relationship.

In 1972, the world soccer championship was held in Mexico. I told a few of my customers that I would probably go to Mexico for the duration of the competition, which lasted about three weeks. It was a very intense meeting of the 32 best teams in the world. But business came first and I did not go after all.

At that time, one particular lady had been coming to my salon for three or four years. She had been recommended by a colleague at work. She always was satisfied with the service she received, but for a long period of time I did not notice her in any particular way. Even now, I can not remember how she looked then.

One day she called me on the telephone and asked if I had gone to the soccer competition. Since she was Hispanic, I thought she was interested in my comments. I told her that I had not been able to go because of business. So we proceeded to have small talk. Toward the end of the conversation, I became bold enough to ask her if she wanted to go out to dinner with me. To my amazement, she said in a very abrupt tone, "Not on my dime," and hung up. It was a very interesting answer and one which I was not used to. As soon as she hung up the telephone, I redialed and asked her if she wanted to go to dinner with me. She said yes. I do not remember where we went, but we decided we would continue to see each other.

Our next meeting was quite interesting. It was after the business day was over, but I still had to prepare financial papers for my CPA. While I was putting everything together, she came to the salon. I excused myself and told her I was not ready because I had to finish the financial papers. She watched me struggle over the calculator. I was typing with one finger, and, of course, that took some time. During my struggle, she asked me several times if she could help. However, being male, I had to do it myself. In addition, I did not think that she could put it together for me.

After a while, I could see that the beautiful lady was getting impatient. She might not have been impatient, but that is how it looked to me. She asked one more time if she could help and I jumped at the offer. To my amazement, she started to use her five fingers on the calculator and she put the package together in no time flat. I did not know then that she was a CPA. Even to this day, we remember this moment with warm hearts.

We continued to go out for a while and I discovered that this lady was smart, educated, and secure. It was something new for me. I felt very comfortable around her and I began to see a new world where money and business had no power

On evening I was in my house in Ravinia and this wonderful lady was living in DesPlaines, a suburb of Chicago. We talked on the telephone for a very long time, and after a while, there was no response from her. I started to worry, so I decided to jump into my Corvette and investigate the situation. It was about eleven at night and I lived about forty-five minutes from DesPlaines. By this time, our relationship was such that I knew where she lived and I had been in her house several times. When I arrived, I was concerned about getting into the house without her knowledge. When I went up the stairs and opened her bedroom door, she was sleeping with the phone to her ear. I do not remember what I did next. However, while I was driving back home, I left the highway twice and drove into the grass because I had fallen asleep while driving.

My life was starting to change. All of a sudden, some things that had been important lost their value. I was not sure what was happening, but I could not get this woman out of my head. As our relationship grew, she told me that she was divorced and that she had five children. The problem was that her ex-husband was forcing himself into her life and was interfering with her children.

The prospect of being involved with five children did not have a negative impact on me. Actually, I had a certain positive feeling about it. Getting a family all at once felt good. However, I knew that easy it was not going to be. I was surprised that I was not fazed at all with the idea of gaining five children at once. Something about this woman was very comfortable so I was not worried.

During our courtship, I found her to be very intelligent. We could talk about anything: music, business, theater, and more. Two things that I liked very much about her were her smile and her intellect. After about five months of courtship, I decided to commit myself to the family life and I gave her a diamond ring. Her children were all happy about the event. The family celebrated our future union at the La Margarita restaurant.

It was the start of yet another life of mine. However, this time I had no experience. Teamwork was going to be the main goal.

Alleluia.

Part Three

FAMILY
FORTITUDE
FULFILLMENT

Chapter 23

This might sound like a disclaimer. However, I want to say that this chapter about my family is how I see it. I am sure that my wife and some of the children might have totally different perspectives.

After trying very hard to be successful in America, I fell in love. All of a sudden, the rest of my endeavors were not as important any more. After being with my wife for a while, I realized that my values were out of proportion. When I was immersed in affluent neighborhoods, I lost the values that I had in Europe. I often said that if anyone gave me a choice between $1,000 and my friends while I was living in Europe, my friends had no price. However, after I had been in the United States for several years, I would have taken the money. I did not realize I had become such a person until I met my wife.

I was surprised about this discovery. I was also a bit confused. I wondered if my business record were clean or whether it had been tainted by my greed. After some pondering, I decided that what was done could not be changed. Instead, I promised myself to be as clean and right about my life from then on.

My wife's name is Carolina III. Like everything else about her, this name has an interesting story behind it. Carolina III was born in Reynosa, Tamaulipas, Mexico. She came from an ancestry that believed very much in women's equality. Her father, Manuel Ortiz, was the great-grandson of a Spanish family. It has been said that the family name, Chapa, originated in the Canary Islands. Manuel's grandmother, Zenona Chapa, married Santos Ortiz a local common man. As a result, her parents disinherited her.

Their son, Trinidad Ortiz, was a veterinarian and a horse trainer for the Mexican army. He married Juliana Gonzalez, whose father was Antonio Gonzalez. Trinidad fathered five children with his first wife, Eusebia Villarreal, in Matamoros, Tamaulipas. After Eusebia's death, his second wife, Urbana Mireles, from Brownsville, Texas, bore him six children.

Manuel, my wife's father, had a partnership with the son of President Plutarco Elias Calles in a private investigation office in Monterrey, Nuevo Leon. Manuel moved to Tampico, Tamaulipas, where he worked for his uncle, General Francisco Gonzalez, the mayor of Tampico, as warden in the Andonegui prison.

My wife's mother, Carolina II de la Cuesta, was the great-granddaughter of the descendents of three brothers named de la Cuesta. Their name came from de la Cuesta de Castilla, who emigrated from Spain to Veracruz. Carolina II's grandfather, Miguel de la Cuesta, had several siblings. One was Adela de la Cuesta, who married General Mier y Teran. His picture is displayed in the Goliad Museum in Texas, since he was in command of the Mexican troops that participated on behalf of the government of President Porfirio Diaz during one of the conflicts with the United States.

Carolina II's father was Jose Miguel de la Cuesta. One of his sisters, Aminta de la Cuesta Calderon, had a son, Arturo Calderon, a student in the Naval Academy in Veracruz. He participated in defending Veracruz during one of the U.S. invasions.

Another sister, Debora de la Cuesta, married Julio Montero, a professor at the University in Veracruz. After his death, a street was named in his honor. Her father married Carolina I Atienza. Her mother, Luz Mora, was later divorced and raised Carolina I, five siblings, and an adopted child.

Carolina II, was fully supported by both parents. They relocated to Mexico City from Orizaba so she could attend the Universidad Nacional Autonoma de Mexico, where she was one of the first women in Mexico to obtain a DDS and go on to practice dentistry.

Carolina III was baptized Maria Carolina de Guadalupe in Monterrey, Nuevo Leon. She was presented for baptism by General Emilio N. Acosta and his wife, Guadalupe Elizondo. Carolina II de la Cuesta and Manuel Ortiz moved to Mexico City when Carolina III was ready to start kindergarten. Carolina III was very talented. She studied ballet and Mexican folkloric dancing for seven years and attended the Escuela Nacional de

Danza in Bellas Artes. She also took seven years of piano, two years of swimming, five years of English, and one year of oratory.

Carolina III attended the Universidad Nacional Autonoma de Mexico, where she received her BS in Humanities and Social Sciences. She also attended the Facultad de Jurisprudencia for three years. Then she studied psychology at the Facultad de Filosofia y Letras.

A short time after Miguel's death, Carolina III's Godfather, General Emilio Acosta, took her to see his best friend Gerardo Murillo, who had just had one leg amputated. Gerardo Murillo, also known as Dr. Atl, was one of the most well-known Mexican writers and painters. The name *Dr. Atl* means *drop of water* in the Aztec dialect Nauatel. A statue honoring Dr. Atl stands in the big plaza in Guadalajara, Mexico. He is buried in Mexico City at the Rotonda de los Hombres Ilustres.

From the day Dr. Atl met Carolina III, they became very good friends. At the time she was 17 and was involved in dancing. Dr. Atl suggested that she organize a national folkloric dancing group that he would finance. However, because of her young age, she was not able to do so.

Carolina III has some wonderful stories to tell about Dr. Atl. One day when he was standing on a street in Mexico City, he had his back against a wall, crutches under his arms, and his hat in his hand. A woman passing by dropped a few pesos into his hat and said, "Get something to eat, poor man." Dr. Atl's only response was "Thank you." The woman never knew that her life had crossed that of one of Mexico's most famous artists.

Carolina III immigrated to the United States in 1953. After having five children, she attended Northwestern University in Chicago, where she studied accounting and became a CPA.

Before I met Carolina III, I was very ambiguous about marriage. I did not feel secure about marrying because I did not feel that I could get support when support was needed. I am not sure why I had that feeling. Maybe it was related to the clientele I was dealing with. They were affluent, but very bored with their lives.

When I met Carolina, I felt something positive happen. The ambiguity disappeared and I felt good about the relationship. I liked her smile and her intellect. She became my best friend and my best of everything.

We were married on May 15, 1971. It was a small wedding with mostly my wife's friends as witnesses. My best man was the husband of another of her friends. After a while, they became good friends of ours. Since the wife was a typical Jewish mother figure, from then on, I called her "Mother." She was a wonderful person and had a tremendous sense of humor.

My life changed completely when I married Carolina. Some people might think that the changes were of confinement and responsibilities. In the dictionary, responsibility is described as being accountable, having an obligation, and being able to distinguish right from wrong. I did not find myself in any of these descriptions. When I do something, it is because I want to do it and I enjoy working through it. The right-from-wrong definition may not be the right description for me. I was told often that anyone in his right mind would run away from a woman with five children. But being a stepfather to five children made me feel proud. However, I did not like the word *stepfather*. It made me feel that I was a stranger, so I never used that word. As far as I was concerned, I was a father.

For our honeymoon, Carolina and I went to Covington, Kentucky. The first evening, we decided to go out to eat, so we dressed to the "T" and drove off to look for a restaurant. After driving for some time, we realized that everything was closed. Covington was not a big city. Back at the hotel, we learned that in Covington everything closes at 9 p.m.. Because the hotel management knew we were newly-weds, they provided us with sandwiches. Just imagine us, dressed to the "T" and eating sandwiches in our hotel room.

The next day was much better. We went to Louisville to bet on the Kentucky Derby. This was a new experience on how to choose a winner. I had always read the race information in the papers so I could pretend that I knew something. But Carolina waited until the horses paraded in front of us. When the last horse passed by, she said to me, "I like this one and this one and that other one. Here is the money. Buy a trifecta." I don't remember if I bet on any other horse because I was still bewildered by her choices. When the race was over, she was $300 ahead. Later on, I tried her system without any positive result. We must have had a wonderful time because we still remember our honeymoon with humor.

My life definitely changed. It was like being in a whirlwind. Things were happening, but I did not have any control. I did not have any plans for the future, so I decided to manage each situation as it arrived. Everything was different: food, environment, and a mother-in-law. The food I was introduced to was great. It was nothing I could find in a restaurant. Everything seemed to be thrown together, a little bit of this and a little bit of that, but it was very good. This changed my diet which had been composed mostly of meat and potatoes. For the first time I tasted tortillas and tacos. I learned that there were corn and flour tortillas, shredded meat dishes, and thin steaks just like in Europe. Not only did I marry a wonderful woman, I also invited myself to a feast.

My mother-in-law, Carolina II, was a nice person. She was working at J. C. Penney's and helping my wife with the children. From time to time, we had short conversations in French. Carolina II knew French because when she was studying dentistry, all the books were in written in French. She was a very humble woman, but very opinionated about most everything. When I was having a conversation with her, I was careful not to get into an argument. Our conversations were simple and non-argumentative. When I wanted to discuss something of a controversial nature, my wife was the person to handle it. My relationship with my mother-in-law was friendly and respectful.

After I married Carolina, I decided that to change my line of work. At the time my back hurt when I had to stand for long periods. This was a long-term result of my track-and-field injury when I was attending Ecole St. Augustin. Since standing was a must for hairstyling, my back problem was a good excuse for making the decision to leave that profession.

Over the years, I went on to a few positions with different companies. After working for myself for a long time, it was difficult for me to adjust to receiving orders, especially those that I disagreed with. However, my business experience helped me adapt to almost any situation.

One of my most interesting positions was in the biggest manufacturing consulting business. First, I had the opportunity to travel again. Second, I had not realized how very important decisions were often made by people who are not equipped to take that responsibility. After a short time, someone must have decided that I was important to the company since I was asked to run their office in Paris. The trouble was that I was married and no one in my family, including myself, wanted to move, so I resigned my position.

The second experience working for someone else was in the fashion business. Even though eventually I worked for several companies, the job as buyer was about the same. I was responsible for a budget and I needed to go to the fashion markets with my buyers. It was a challenging and comfortable situation for me since I had been involved for short periods of time with my dad's business. Over the years, I was buyer for goods that included lingerie, dresses, sportswear, winter clothing, and furs. I attended the major fashion markets in New York, Chicago, Dallas, and Los Angeles.

The market always has funny moments. Some of those moments I will never forget. When I was a buyer, a handshake with the manufacturer or his representative was like a contract. My word was very important and that's how I built my reputation. After a short time, I was known and respected for that reputation. It is no secret that most of the fashion market is run by Jews. Since I am half Jewish, it was easy for me to build friendships in most of the businesses. When the market became aware of my ancestry, doors opened naturally.

Working in the fashion industry was good, but I later stumbled upon an opportunity to work for the State of Texas. It was a very interesting situation for me since I never before worked for such an entity. For seven years, I worked as a bureaucrat. It was certainly very different from what I was used to. I had never heard about minimum standards. Who could be comfortable with that proposition? However, I found out that minimum standards were like golden rules. As always, I adjusted. But I never became part of any team because I was too much on the border-line between those minimum standards and "Let's do better!"

Now Carolina and I are retired, but we still work part time to keep our sanity. God gave us comparatively good health and we are thankful for that. Who knows what will happen when health leaves us?

Upon reflection, my question is, "Did I make a difference in our lives in general, in our children's lives, or in anything at all?"

Chapter 24

THE CHILDREN'S CHALLENGES

Carolina III and I were married on May 15, 1971. We decided to live in Carolina's house since it was a symbol of her persistence in acquiring a mortgage. At that time, it was not easy for a single woman or for a woman with children to secure any type of mortgage. It was really a *tour de force* that she was able to buy the two-story duplex with a small backyard.

With marriage came five children. The youngest one was ten and the oldest was 18. When I first joined the family, I drove the children to meet their biological father for their Wednesday visits at a restaurant. I sat at a table away from them until the visit was over. During those visits, he made his point to the children that Victor, the oldest one, was still the man of the house. The children were always more difficult to handle after these visits, because they were placed in a no-win situation. They were told one story while they visited with their biological father. Then they saw different ways at home that did not fit with what they had been told.

In my opinion, they were also very confused because they were living with us and visiting their father. It seemed that the burden for them was to please both sides and, of course, that was not possible. They also had an understandable affinity for their father, regardless of his actions. He was abusive toward their mother, who was very good at hiding her feelings from everyone.

In my eyes, Victor had a tough time having another man in the house, while his dad was put in a secondary position in his eyes. At the time, I did not know how to tell him that it was not his fault. It was very difficult for me to judge how to handle the situation. I could feel his resistance, but I did not know how to disarm it. It seemed that the family on his father's side had a lot of hold on him, even though most of the family lived in Mexico and sometimes visited the United States.

Victor was very sensitive about how people viewed him. He seemed to want to be accepted by his peers and he wanted to please all his friends. His philosophy in dealing with problems was interesting. He thought that most every physical situation that needed to be solved had mind-over-matter solutions. Victor and I had casual conversations on many occasions. Some were better than others. Sometimes those conversations ended on a negative note. As a teenager close to adulthood, Victor had the usual growing-up problems. His mood changed from day to day, so my relationship with him was in his control. I tried to react to him rather than force the issues.

While we were living in Carolina's home, which we later called the old house, Victor was a senior in high school. It was fun to go and see him participate in soccer and in his preferred discipline, track and field. He was very good and for the mile run, he always was tops. Victor had a lot of friends and most of the time over the weekends, they played in our basement where we had a ping-pong table, a small pool table, and a card table. Victor was very good at games and he even invented some. My wife and I liked the arrangement because we knew where he was.

After being married for a while, Carolina and I decided to move and to build a new house in a different neighborhood. For us, moving would be cutting the umbilical cord with the past. It was an exciting time for me. We were building a house for a family of seven. What a change!

We sold the house where the family had been living and went to our new future. Sleeping on the floor on a mattress was very new for me. Since our house was not finished on time, we had to sleep in a house the builder lent us. It was kind of fun for a while, but everybody wanted to move as fast as possible into our own home in Schaumburg. The town of 6,000 had a small pond with swans. The school district seemed to be good. Our house was in a new community where a new high school was to be built.

After we moved to the new house, and a semblance of order existed, real life took over. I was not sure what my role should be or how I should exercise my fatherly duty, if such a thing existed. In my mind, I knew I needed to be involved in the children's lives without being seen as an intruder. The only experience I had was that education and discipline were very important in anyone's life. So I decided that the education of the children would be my focus.

The discipline was a little more delicate. The most difficult situations occurred when the children did not give respect to their mother. Sometimes, they talked to her with disrespect and I felt that I needed to mediate. That often strained relations with both sides. I felt that when they did not respect their mother, they did not respect me. Many times, my wife asked me to leave the discipline to her, but that was easier said than done.

At the time, the family had three teenagers and two wannabes. I had to deal with two important factors. The first was very sensitive because their biological father was still involved in their lives. The involvement was not necessarily because he cared. In my opinion, it was more to show the children that no matter what their mother did, he was still the man of the family. I might be wrong and some of the children might argue this point. However, his womanizing while he was married pointed to the contrary. His second marriage was handled the same way, even though he did not get divorced again. At first, I disliked the man, but later I felt sorry for him. Carolina III was such a good person, but he could not see that.

In the new house, I also made an attempt to interest the children in different types of music and different television shows. I did not get much cooperation. My feeble efforts were not good enough. My problem was to gauge when to insist and when to let go. Most of the time, I let go so that the home atmosphere would be relaxed.

Soon Victor was ready to go to college, about a two- or three-hour drive from the new house. It was an ambiguous situation. On one hand, there might be less dissension at home. But on the other hand, I wanted to have more time to know him better and reach him.

When Carolina and I visited him at college, he seemed to be doing well. He found two cats in the wild and took them to his dorm. However, when he met his girlfriend, the cats changed domicile and ended up with us. Those cats stayed with us for over 20 years until they died.

At Christmas when Victor came home from college, we were all settled into our new house. By then, his grades were not the best. He and I had a short talk about the need of education and I have to say that from then on, he was very successful in his studies.

My goal was to make education the most important criteria with the children. My philosophy was that they had to work to their capacity, no matter what that capacity was. The way that I explained my philosophy to the children was perhaps childish, but I wanted them to understand that whether their capacity was A, B or C, then that was what I expected of them.

Very often Victor and I did not see things the same way, but there was a mutual respect between us. To this day, I wish that we could have a better relationship, like that between father and son. Our conversations are usually just small talk and about sports, but nothing about deeper feelings or matters.

Victor does call me Dad and I am glad that he does. I don't want to speculate the why he calls me Dad, but maybe neither of us knows how to resolve the situation. I think I know that he has an idea what a father should be, but we might not agree. But it doesn't matter. He is a good dad to his children and that's what counts the most. I have to say that as far as Victor's being a man and a father to his children, I am very proud of him. I don't know if I had anything to do with his success, but I know my wife probably did. Victor turned out to be a good and caring person.

While living in Schaumburg, Carolina mentioned several times that she would enjoy living in Texas. I did not pay much attention to this request because we both had our careers in the Chicago area. Winter came and every morning Mario and I shoveled snow from our long driveway. One night I came home late from my office. I was driving the Datsun convertible, which was a gift from my wife. When I arrived in front of our house, I noticed that our driveway, which Mario and I had shoveled earlier, was blocked by about two feet of snow, a gift left by the city's snowplow. I decided to run through it with my car. To my frustration, the car ended up balancing precariously on top of the two feet of frozen snow. Needless to say, I was not happy.

When I saw Carolina that night, I said, "You want to go to Texas? Let's go now." Since my wife and I are gypsies, my suggestion was not out of the ordinary. The children, who were attending school, were not thrilled, but when the decision was made, there was no recourse. We decided to sell our assets and prepare for the move.

I contacted a friend who worked in Dallas for an executive search firm. I indicated to him that I was going to move to Texas with the family and that I needed some help in finding a position. I was ready to change professions, but I still wanted to work in retail. A short time later, I had a meeting with a man who was looking for a number-two person to run his business. I will call him Mr. Kirsh. We met in Chicago at the McCormick

Building where the houseware show was held. By the end of the meeting, we had agreed on the conditions that would allow me and my family move to Laredo, Texas.

My wife and I decided that I should go first, while she took care of the disposal of our assets. So I packed my sports car and I went on my way. I had an excellent trip. However, when I reached the last segment from San Antonio to Laredo, a funny feeling engulfed me. While I was driving with the top down, a pick-up truck with a gun hanging in the back window passed me.

"Wow!" I said to myself. "I could get shot for no reason at all and no one would find me." I was not used to driving 150-plus miles without seeing a house, a gas station, or any other cars. It was not like being in the Chicago area, where the only way I knew that I had passed from one village to another was by reading the signs on the side of the road.

When Carolina joined me in Laredo, we decided to build another house. It was a beautiful one with five bedrooms, the maid's quarters for our live-in maid, living room, dining room, and bar. The swimming pool took up most of the back yard, which also had palm and banana trees. Victor visited us before the cement block wall around the property was finished. One night I heard some loud noises, so I took a baseball bat and went to the back of the house. While I going around the corner, I saw a shadow coming toward me. I was ready to hit the shadow with my baseball bat when I realized that Victor was coming from the other side.

When Victor saw me, he pointed to the pool where two cows were swimming. The cows had come from an adjacent field and in through the unfinished wall. It was about 2 a.m. by then, and I decided to call the Laredo police to send someone to take care of the cows. When I explained that two cows were in my swimming pool, the police officer said, "Sure. We will send someone right away." I told Carolina, "I am sure they thought I was drunk. No one will come." Victor agreed with me, so we chased the cows out by ourselves. The next morning I was in front of the house when a police car drove slowly towards me. The officer asked, "Are you the one with the cows in the swimming pool?"

The whole Laredo work episode seemed just like the movie *The Godfather*. After getting comfortable in my executive position, I took part in a ritual every morning. Mr. Kirsh and I met in a huge office with a very long table. He sat on one end, while I sat at the other end just as he suggested. Before our meeting started, he called important people in Laredo and told them what to do. Those included the sheriff, the newspaper editor, the mayor, and others. When he finished with the calls, our meeting was over. I realized that he did that just to show me how powerful he was.

We stayed in Laredo about two years. Then we decided that we'd better exit this milieu before it was too late. Several years later, I learned that Mr. Kirsh's new home was jail. I did not know exactly why, but I had an idea. I wonder how a man who was at that time worth over $50 million needed to be dishonest.

We moved to Corpus Christi, Texas, where we built another house by the Gulf of Mexico. The house had two wooden decks, one on the upper level, and one on the first floor. I could fish from either of the decks. Victor joined us in Corpus Christi. At the time, he was married and he was teaching in a Catholic school. In Texas, he became father of two beautiful children, Luke and Anna. Now his children are in their early twenties. I remember having fun with them when they were small.

One day Luke, who was about two or three, was fishing with me from the deck. I remember he was very happy to be by the water and to have a fishing pole in his hands. All of a sudden, he felt a fish on the line and tried to get our attention because the fish was pulling him into the water. It is normal to try to hold on, and that's what Luke did. With some help from his grandpa, he held the pole in his hands. The fish was not as lucky. Luke caught it and we enjoyed eating it later that day.

Luke's younger sister Anna had a very strong will and was determined to achieve anything. She was very competitive and still is. Anything her brother did, she did as well, but she tried to do it better. Anna even challenged me to run against her a short race. I do not remember who won, but that wasn't important. It was fun to see her joyous nature. Those are nice memories, but the pragmatic life took over and the children grew up.

Lourdes was our oldest girl and the second oldest among the children. When I became part of the family, she was already having problems with my wife. I tried to talk and communicate with her, but I had no success. She was very close to her maternal grandmother, Carolina II, who had returned to Mexico by that time. Lourdes asked to go live with her and soon she joined her grandmother. Since she was bilingual, she found a good job in the city.

While in Mexico City, Lourdes got married. My wife decided not to go to the wedding for personal reasons. I do not remember much about Lourdes besides the few battles she had with us. As a CPA, Carolina was always trying to teach Lourdes how to save money when she was working.

I don't remember if Lourdes changed her last name to Nirenberger or not. I always wondered about her motive in possibly changing her name. However, I know that the relationship between Lourdes and me was never very good. Even now, it is non-existent. On the positive side, in her middle age Lourdes did go to school and graduated in criminal studies. She now works as a member of a sheriff's department in South Texas.

Martha was the next child. She was the quiet one the smallest of all our children, because when she was a toddler, she had rheumatic fever. She was a beautiful girl and very much grown-up for her age. She had shoulder-length black hair framing her well-defined face. She had a smile that I am sure melted the hearts of a few boys in high school, but they did not know how to approach her. Martha was the most serious of the children. I remember that she was hardly ever in any difficulties. Since I rarely had to reprimand her, the other children were convinced that she was my preferred child.

I certainly tried to explain to the children that there is a difference between *love* and *like*. I always told them that I loved them all the same way and that there was no preferred child. However, I also said that to like someone is to accept the behaviors and values that you can identify with. Of course, I did not know then and I was not told that I did not reach first base with my explanation. Now I understand that they had a very good reason to think that Martha was my preferred child. Besides loving her as a parent, I also liked her very much because she behaved and did the right things.

In school Martha did not have many friends. I heard that she was viewed as a snob. She did not have boyfriends, probably because of their feeling that she was too good. In my view, all this was a misreading of her by the other students. I am sure she had few girlfriends, but I really don't remember since she did not bring them home. When we were living in the old house, she did have a best girlfriend and they were like sisters.

For her age, Martha was very poised and thoughtful. The girls took turns shopping and cooking for the entire family. When it was her turn, Martha was always very responsible with the money. She always looked for bargains, which sometimes made for humorous moments during dinnertime.

After a while, Martha decided to call me Dad. I was very proud of that. For some time we had a very good relationship. After graduating from high school, she went to junior college for two years and received an associate's degree. By then, Martha had a best friend named Coleen.

They were very close and when our family decided to move to South Texas, Martha asked if she could stay in Chicago with her friend. Later they came to visit us in South Texas. It was nice to see them both again.

It might sound as though Martha could not do anything wrong, but in fact she was not an angel. She had her own problems while growing up. However, she faced her dilemmas and solved her problems. After she got married, each time we visited her in a North Chicago suburb, I had a very funny feeling that she was avoiding me. Every time I called her my daughter, I detected a wall between us. At first I thought I was imagining things. I mentioned it to my wife and we decided that I was wrong. However, after few more visits, I realized that it was true.

During one visit, Martha told me that she was not going to call me Dad anymore. That was her prerogative. I cannot say that I was not hurt, but I did not have any control over this situation. After a while, I decided that since I was not her dad anymore, I would consider her an acquaintance of mine. Some people would say that it is a bizarre position to take. However, it was my prerogative. Maybe it was my way of preserving my feelings, which may be normal. I know that I have no regrets about my decision.

Mario was the fourth child. When I became part of his life, he was 12. He was a funny little guy with a very strong work ethic. He delivered newspapers very early in the morning before going to school. Sometimes I went with him on his route.

On the day of our wedding, both Mario and Dora were in the car and he asked me if he could call me Dad. I was honored that he asked me and, of course, I said yes. It did not last very long. The next day he changed his mind.

Mario was a character. When he came into a room, his personality engulfed the whole place. He had a million-dollar smile. I am sure that while he was living with us, he told us many stories that we believed at the time, but that might not have been true. I remember that when we were living in our new house, we had grass that needed to be cut. Mario was ready to cut the neighbor's grass for free while ours got longer and longer. Sometimes he raced me on his bicycle. We had for some time a very close relationship.

Mario wore glasses. Without them, he could not see very well. He also had a very good sense of humor. One day in Texas, when he was driving his grandmother to the store, he had to stop at a traffic light.

While waiting for the red light to change, he said, "Grandma, when you see the green light, let me know."

As a young student, Mario was average. Going into his teenage years, his behavior was exciting. For my wife and me, vigilance was in order. Yet, he had such a great personality that it was hard to really get upset at him. I have good memories of when Mario was a young boy. One night when we were still in our old house, his mother asked him to go to bed. We did not follow him to his room. After a while, we found him sleeping in the middle of the stairway that led to his bedroom.

Despite ups and downs during his tender years, Mario grew up to be a good person. He always tried to be straight-forward in his relationships. As a father, he was very close to his two daughters. They loved him and looked up to him. Years later, they became successful in their own lives. The relationship between us remains cordial. I enjoy visiting with his family. Mario is always very gracious during those visits. Even during conversations when we do not agree, he respects our differences of opinion.

To this day, Mario still has the wonderful personality that all his friends and neighbors enjoy. He is able to make friends anywhere. The only regret I have about Mario is that our conversations are either small talk or very superficial. I do not remember having a serious talk with Mario as I imagine a father and son have. Of course, I am not a father to him, so I can understand why. Still, the fact is that at times I miss that relationship. When I am in that state of mind, I tell myself that I did not marry the children; I married my wife.

The fifth child was Dora. When we got married she was ten years old. After the wedding was over, she was crying. I cannot remember why, but I know it was not because she was upset. While she and her brother Mario were in the car, she asked if she could call me Dad. To this day she still calls me Dad and I consider her like my own child.

While she was growing up, Dora certainly gave us enough headaches. For some reason, she was often angry at someone. A lot of times it was her older brothers whom she felt were always telling her what to do. She was not afraid of anyone. She was a challenge, not only to us, but also to her brothers. One day she and one of her brothers were having a strong argument which was very close to becoming a boxing match. I suppose that she felt threatened because the only thing that I remember is that she told him, "Go ahead and try!" while she elevated her chin and dared him to hit her. She was a package to handle.

One of Dora's complains was that no one listened to her, so the only thing she could do was kick the dog. We had a mutt named Snoopy who was not very brave, but he was very loving. I made fun of him because when the door bell rang, he dashed under one of the children's bed and only then started to bark. I don't remember very much how Dora was in the old house, probably because I was busy getting acclimated to the family and I had other matters were on my mind. In the new house, when I felt more part of the family, I started to pay better attention to most of the kids.

Dora took a lot of our time because of her behavior. She often seemed to work against us. At least that is how it looked to me. When we moved, Dora had to attend a new school, so my wife and I took her by car the day before and showed her how to get back home. It was not far, so she didn't take the school bus. The next day when school ended, she was nowhere to be found. We went looking for her by car. We thought that she might have taken a wrong turn. Around seven o'clock, she still was not home and we really started to get worried.

At 7:30 a car stopped in front of our house and Dora was home. School had ended at three o'clock and until seven she was walking around lost. She stopped at a gasoline station and told the owner that she was lost and could not call us because we did not have a telephone in the new house yet. The owner of the station asked her for her address and gave her a ride home. She was scared because she accepted a ride from a stranger and she thought that we might get mad at her.

Even though Dora was contrary to almost anything, I had good times with her. One summer the family went to Florida to visit some friends. We rented a bungalow by the sea. The weather was beautiful. I remember getting up at 4 a.m. and within a few steps, I was sitting on the pier watching the sun rise and the pelicans flying and fishing. It was amazing to me how the pelicans dove to catch the fish without hurting themselves. It was very quiet and I could hear the splash when the pelicans hit the water. To my astonishment, Dora came and sat with me and enjoyed the moment. It was the first time that I felt that she cared for me and the feeling was very much reciprocated. I felt good because someone else was enjoying the same thing. During the following days, Dora joined me in the early mornings and I relished those moments.

Another time we were ready to travel from Chicago to Washington, D.C. on vacation. The whole family, except Victor, was going. We had a big Lincoln that could accommodate everyone, even my father who was visiting from Paris. Dora was not on her best behavior. While we were dealing with Dora, everyone else was ready to go. Finally, my wife and I decided to leave Dora behind. That decision was very unpopular, mostly with my dad. He declared that if Dora was not going, he would stay with her.

Obviously, we were headed in the wrong direction. When my father visited, he always took the kids' side, especially Dora's. I think that when Dora saw that my dad was in her corner, she decided to get into the car. However, this incident started a lively discussion between my dad and me to such an extent that he threatened to get out of the car while it was in transit. I have to say that after that storm, calm took over and we all enjoyed our vacation.

Dora's education was very important to me. She had some problem understanding fractions, so I took it upon myself to help her. I have to say that at the time I did not have much patience. My wife would say that I still don't. After explaining fractions to Dora for a while, I realized that progress was not coming. As a last resort, I decided to use fruits as props for the fractions. I cut the fruits into many different pieces, reconstructed the fruits, and explained with the fruit the words *numerator* and *denominator*. But I felt that I was still not making any progress. Actually, I was getting angry, which was not a good example to set for a young child.

At one point, I even cut a fruit in half and in desperation I asked this little girl, "Which half is bigger?" That was not very smart coming from a grown-up who was supposed to be a dad. At the end, however, I think she understood how fractions work. Since then, whenever anyone in the family mentions the phrase *fruit salad*, fractions come to mind.

Dora grew up to be a very fine person and a lovely daughter. She was a math teacher for ten years. I hope I had a positive influence upon her. When her mother or I had any physical problems that needed hospitalization, she was always there for us. I asked her and others in the family to write some memories for this book about life when I joined the family. Only Dora decided to participate.

In the following chapter, *On the Radar,* Dora shares some of her feelings about life with her dad.

Chapter 25

*M*any people believe I should have run the other way when faced with acquiring an instant family, but I must say that am proud to be a husband and a dad. Here, in "On The Radar," my daughter Dora M. Mata describes her memories of our family.

I find myself reflecting at the age of 46 about who I am today versus who I was at the age of 10, when Dad became my dad. I feel very confident, with high self-esteem, and proud of the person I have become. In retrospect, I wonder how I feel this way today when I didn't have any of those traits at the age of 10. The conclusion follows in the next several paragraphs.

My mother is someone to be proud of as she was a single mother of five rather difficult children. She often had to assume the role of our father due to the financial struggles she faced frequently. Being a single mother from 1963 until 1971 during an era where divorce wasn't common at all was a situation none of us will ever completely comprehend. I know that she was often busy trying to make ends meet on a budget where most would just throw their hands up in the air in desperation. Additionally, she was doing all of this in the suburbs of Chicago where single, Hispanic mothers were not your next-door neighbors.

Therefore, being the youngest of my sibling group of five, I often remember being more bonded with my maternal grandmother who had unselfishly left her profession as a dentist in Mexico in order to help her only child raise her five children during this very difficult time.

I frequently wish that I had more vivid memories of my mother when I was growing up, but I don't, probably because I wasn't the one who needed that much attention when many of my siblings were either teens or rapidly approaching those teen years. In my mother's eyes, she had more on her plate than any of us will ever really understand.

When Dad became my dad, he put me on the radar. I don't believe he really knew that he was doing that for me, since I really didn't know that he was doing that for me either. I reached that conclusion as an adult after I reflected on my childhood. I don't remember having any personal time with any adults when I was growing up, except for my grandmother and I cherish those memories.

However, in 1970, when my mother introduced us to my dad-to-be, I remember his taking us to carnivals, dinner, and other events that included only me and my mom, sometimes only me. How will I ever forget those moments when I never had any moments like that prior to Dad's joining our family? Many times it didn't seem that great, since along with those wonderful memories came the long discussions about who I was and who I wanted to be and why was I so self-destructive and angry. How was I, at that early age, ever going to be able to answer any of those questions when I really didn't understand the questions?

I was academically behind in school, so much so that I never ever thought that academics were ever going to be an extension of my life. Because I was viewed by my peers as a "poor, dirty Spic," my self-esteem was very poor. I had one best friend, Jamie, whom I always recall because she was a true friend when others mostly bullied me. So there weren't many good memories during my early elementary years.

We moved to a new neighborhood after my mom and dad married in 1971, so everything was better, right? Well, not exactly. I remember attending a new school where nobody would know my early years and I believed that everything would just work itself out. So I changed my name from Dora to Madelyn because I thought that was such a beautiful name.

I was determined to do well in school because I didn't want to be put into the buzzard's reading group and other under-achieving groups that I had always been placed into in my previous school. I even remember that I wanted to be the smartest student in my class. What I didn't understand was how academically behind I was in school. Therefore, that goal wasn't a realistic goal simply because I moved 30 miles away and was attending a new school. Although I had good intentions, I wasn't going to will it to happen. I guess shortly after I realized that it wasn't going to happen, I went back to the person I knew best with the low self-esteem and lack of confidence. I even returned to Dora rather than the made-up nickname I gave myself, Madelyn.

I remember Dad always trying to stay involved in my studies and I knew how disappointed he was going to be when he realized how far behind I was in school. He never mentioned it to me, but I knew he had to know. Many times he would have me read from my text books. If I didn't comprehend what I was reading, which was frequently, I would make up my own stories so that when we engaged in the discussions of what I had read, I could answer his questions.

That was all good for the classes that had a lot of reading, but what was I going to do in the arithmetic classes? Well, it wasn't that bad, as math had always been my strongest subject. I'm not indicating that I was even near grade level, but I definitely felt more comfortable doing math than reading anything. Therefore, I believe that math was easier for me to catch up than any subject that involved reading. The endless fruit salads, which Dad described in the previous chapter, helped me understand fractions to the point that I caught up quickly in that subject area. I caught up so much that by the eighth grade, I became the class clown in my math class, since I didn't have to listen to the teacher to understand the subject area we were taught. I had finally found a way to fit in rather than to be an outcast.

I recall my dad always telling me he was going to send me to boarding school if I didn't stay focused on school. What he and my mother didn't know was that only made me act up more, as I wanted to go away to school. I couldn't imagine that being a punishment. I always wanted to be smart and if going away to school was going to help me accomplish that goal, then I was all for it, but I wasn't going to tell my parents that was what I wanted.

I have very great memories with Dad, who would take me to run errands with him. I even was able to go with him to the Market when he was the buyer for a clothing store. I remember seeing outfits for children in my age bracket and wishing that I could have pretty clothes like the ones at the Market, because prior to Dad's becoming my dad I had to wear a lot of previously-worn clothing from my sisters or my godmother's daughter, Angie. But we were always taught not to ask for something so those thoughts would rapidly perish.

I will never forget the Datsun Midget that Dad loved. I remember driving through downtown Chicago where he would randomly start waving his hands in the air and exclaiming that life was great. I would slip as far down in the passenger seat as I could just to not be seen, but more importantly to not be recognized by anyone. For once, I was somebody and I was on the radar.

I'll never forget Grandpa, who visited annually from France and who didn't speak English. Oh, I didn't speak French, but I always felt connected to him and I never felt that not speaking a common language was a barrier for us. Grandpa was always on my side, no matter what I did or said. Grandpa wasn't going to allow anyone to leave me behind or make me sad. Grandpa always gave me money when Mom and Dad weren't looking. On a daily basis while he was visiting, he would give me $20. I remember telling him the best I could that I still had the $20 that he gave me the previous day and he would just tell me to put it away and that it was for ME. That is not where it ended either. On his last day he slipped me a $100 bill and the more I said, "No, I can't take this," the more he assured me in his way that I could keep what he gave me because it was his to give. That's when shopping at the Hallmark Store for stickers and silly things that I didn't need began. But, I was able to buy them and nobody could take them away from me because they didn't know I had it.

The bond I had with Grandpa extended over the years through my adult years. One regret I always will have is that he wanted me to go live with him in France and attend La Sorbonne, one of many do-overs I wish I had in life. I knew I had a special bond with him when he had a stroke and Dad traveled to Paris to see him. He had basically been non-verbal due to the stroke, but Dad told me that he asked about me, as if he believed that I was there with him in Paris.

On August 2, 1987, I recall waking up feeling unusually depressed. It was a day that I shouldn't have felt depressed as it was my first wedding anniversary with my then-husband and we had been looking forward to celebrating it as we had made plans earlier in the week. However, on that morning when I awoke, I had this ugly feeling that I struggled all day to shake off. I only wanted to lie on the couch, watch television, and be left alone by everyone else. I remember dragging myself to the movies, as I had made those plans with my then-husband and I knew I wasn't being fair to him, since he wanted to celebrate our anniversary. But as we sat in the movies, I kept wondering about this feeling I had continued to struggle with all day.

A couple of days later, I received the phone call that my grandfather had passed away on that Sunday, August 2, 1987. As I wept, I realized that we always had a connection and this phenomenal experience confirmed it for me. I went to Grandpa's funeral and I let him know how much he meant to me and how thankful I was that he too had become a part of my life. Communication had never interfered with us. I love you, Grandpa! *Je vous aime*, Grandpa!

It sounds pretty good to be on the radar, huh? Well, it was! However, let me remind you that Dad was an only child who spent most of his childhood either escaping the war or in boarding schools, rather than interacting with large families or learning how to be a part of a family unit. And that was a disaster for many. I guess if we had the do-overs, I wish my dad would have learned how to go from being an only child to an active member of a larger family unit. Unfortunately, Dad didn't have that luxury, since all of a sudden he was the stepfather of five children between the ages of 10–18.

Dad wanted to be a parent to all of us, but he wasn't sure how to go about it. He lacked patience, but as a child, he probably didn't have patience demonstrated to him. He lacked the knowledge on how to bond with my older siblings, since his bonds as a child hadn't been very strong either. I believe it was just easier to bond with me because I was the youngest and all I wanted was to be noticed.

Dad had his own ideas about right and wrong, good and bad, and love and hate. Many times that is all it took for Dad to believe that he loved us, that he was good to us, and that he was always right. I laugh about it now and I wish the rest of my siblings could laugh about it too. Dad was in over his head, but he really didn't know it, so he was never going to acknowledge it. I wonder if he knows it now. With all that is good, there is some bad and that was the bad for me. Dad needed to learn how to parent in the USA in the 1970's, not in the manner that he was parented in Europe in the 1950's. When we have children, we have all those precious memories with our children, beginning with their infancy stage and continuing with each subsequent stage of their childhood. Those precious memories of those earlier stages help us accept the more challenging stages of our children as they approach the difficult pre-teen and teens. Well, my poor dad didn't have those precious memories with any of us. To just become the dad and have to accept all of us for the way we were had to be difficult for him, as it would be for anyone.

I do believe that Dad always said what was on his mind for all the right reasons. But how do you ever as a 10, 11, or 12-year-old fully comprehend what is meant when somebody tells you, "I love you, but I don't I like you." As a 10, 11, or 12-year-old, all I heard was the latter, the negative. Although now I know exactly what he was saying, I didn't then and it only added to my confusion and frustrations that I already had from my earlier years.

Dad has continued to be there for me as an adult since I have had some trying times. That is why I know that he really does love us and he just wants to be loved by us in turn. I struggled with an eating disorder in the late 1990's, and if it hadn't been for my dad, I don't know that I would have ever conquered that disorder. I remember looking in the mirror at my size-1 self and wondering why I still looked so fat. I really believed all I had to do was lose more weight and I would be okay. Well, I am 5' 7" and never was a size 1 in high school. Why did I believe I was fat? That's another story, but my point was that if my dad hadn't gotten me out of bed and taken me to a doctor, I wouldn't be here now.

Thanks, Dad. I love you very much. Thanks for putting me on the radar. Thanks for always believing in me, even when I didn't believe in myself, which was pretty frequently.

Chapter 26

In 1942 my mother and I were living in Berlin, Germany. I discovered that fact through some pictures that I have of my mother and me taking sun on a beach. It was interesting to me that anyone during the war in Poland could be sunbathing on a beach. I found out later that near Berlin, there is a lake with a beach. I also found out that this was where the Nazi elite were living, among them, Hitler, Himmler and others.

After living in Berlin in 1942, my mother and I found ourselves on a train to Auschwitz. I often asked myself how we went from living with the elite to being forced into a free ticket to Auschwitz. Later, my cousin Tad Nowicki gave me some clues, which I wrote described in *Chapter 2, My Mother, Leokadia Mackiewicz.*

I remember the wagon was so crowded that people could not fall or faint because there was no room. On the top four corners of the wagon, there were little rectangular windows. A man, whom my mother did not know, took me on his shoulder so that I could breathe. Without that man's help, I would not have survived the trip.

The train never made it to Auschwitz. It was the only train that was stopped by the Polish Underground. After the train was stopped, I remember that my mother and I ran as fast as we could towards a line of trees where a forest was starting.

Many years later, my wife Carolina and I went to the U.S. Holocaust Memorial Museum in Washington D.C. and I showed her exactly where I had been in the wagon.

My wife and I visited my nephew Frederick Nowicki and his wife Anna in Poland in 2003. It is very interesting to know why Frederick does not have the same last name as I. His grandfather, my paternal uncle, was an economist for the Polish communist government. His boss, who was his friend even though he was a communist, made a request of him. It was not possible for my uncle to work for a communist group when he had a Jewish name, so my uncle then changed his name to Nowicki. During the war, my uncle was part of the Jewish Underground.

Visiting Auschwitz was a slow-motion experience for me. Slow motion was important because I wanted to be immersed in the feeling and the spirit of the place. Above the iron gates at the entrance to the concentration camp is the inscription: *ARBEIT MACHT FREI.* Those words mean "Work will set you free." I could not stop thinking about the ambiguous feelings the prisoners must have experienced. They knew what was going to happen. However, at that moment, they were probably grasping for the hope that maybe they had a chance to survive.

Inside the camp, we visited the different buildings with displays of the eye glasses, shoes, and even hair that had been cut from the victims. There was also a woven sack that resembled a potato sack but was made of human hair. My wife found several large books that documented the deaths of all the prisoners. She looked and found the names of my mother's family. I know that members of my mother's family died in Auschwitz. However, I am not sure those were my relatives.

While I was walking through the buildings, for the first time in my life I had a feeling of belonging. For the first time, I felt part of something bigger than myself. In that moment, I felt part of an entity, but I was not sure what entity. However, I knew that somehow I had things in common with this place and with the next concentration camp, Birkenau.

I tried to imagine what the prisoners had felt, knowing that most of them had their family at Birkenau, just a mile or so away from Auschwitz. They could see the black smoke spewing from chimneys. All the prisoners knew the meaning of the smoke.

I wanted to visit Birkenau. It is there that the train came and unloaded the prisoners. From Birkenau, the prisoners who were chosen to work would march to Auschwitz.

I entered the Birkenau concentration camp on foot under the arch made of bricks. I marched on the rails the trains used. In my mind, I could see the people on the train and hear their screams for help. I could imagine how they were rushed into death and work groups.

The women and the children were mostly directed to the make-believe showers where they were killed. Some of the women and young female children who were able to work were spared, so they marched with the men to Auschwitz. The men and male children who looked strong were directed to a second group for work.

I walked very slowly on the railway platform which was made of sand. I wanted to catch the spirit and the feeling of all these people. While I was walking ever-so-slowly, I noticed that at the far end of the camp there were huge pine trees. The sun was setting and the sun's rays were making a halo around the pine trees. The view was beautiful. I wondered if it were possible that at such terrible moments anyone had even noticed this beauty. Later, I read about this in Eli Weisel's book *Night*. Mr. Wiesel himself is a survivor of the Auschwitz camp and in his book he mentioned the sun's rays flowing through the pine trees and how majestic they looked.

I continued walking towards the pine trees in the direction of the two crematoriums which were in ruins. The Germans, knowing that the Russian Army was not very far away, wanted to destroy evidence before they retreated. However, a floor plan showed the visitors how it was before the destruction. It was easy to see where the prisoners disrobed. Then they were told they had to take showers. Of course, there were no showers. When the victims were in the make-believe showers, the doors were closed and cyanide was dropped through the roof.

I was told many years ago by my cousin Wiesia, who herself was an Auschwitz survivor, that when the doors to the death chamber were opened, the prisoners were piled in a big mound resembling a pyramid. It was said that while they were being gassed, the victims tried to reach the ceiling for air. At the crematorium, there was a room where, after the victims were dead, their gold teeth were extracted and melted. When that operation was finished, the corpses were burned.

I went to the side of one of the crematoriums and saw a big hole full of water. The water was greenish around the border and gray toward the center. There were a few frogs in it. I wondered if any of those frogs were spirits. The hole was made by the Germans to receive the ashes of the dead. The Germans cremated corpses so fast that they had difficulties disposing of the ashes.

When I saw that murky water and accepted its meaning, I felt proud to be half Jewish. Since my father was a Jew and my mother was Catholic, I found myself thinking that I could have been in that hole. What if, I wondered, I had died at Auschwitz? That question intrigued me and I began to see my life in a different perspective. It felt odd to watch something happen and to realize that if I had died, that same thing would happen regardless. For example, if a bird flies by a tree, that bird would fly the same path whether I were dead or alive. However, visiting my best friend is possible only because I am alive. Perhaps this question is only vivid in the minds of people who had an experience with Auschwitz or other concentration camps. But, on reflection, I believe this feeling lies within everyone, but only a few people are cognizant of it.

I still remember the day I discovered the three *krasnoludki* under a shrub. I was only a child, but I understood their message. They indicated that I should not be worried, that nothing would happen to me, and that I would be safe. Now, as I reflect on my life, I do not feel any guilt because I escaped death in Auschwitz. On the contrary, I realize that I belong to a part of history. Maybe this is why I finally feel that I belong to a bigger entity.

Chapter 27

I have often wondered if I have made a difference in this world. My question now, as a senior citizen, is, "Did I make an impact on our children's lives, our lives in general, or on anything at all?"

I have described my World War II experiences — the bombs, the running and the hiding, finally being reunited with my father. But I have not explored one old image that remains strong even today.

Pine trees and their pine cones have been part of my memory since 1942 when the train that was taking my mother and me to Auschwitz never reached its destination. The Polish Underground stopped the train and freed everyone. I remember running as fast as I could from the train into the near-by forest. Even in those circumstances, I recall the quietness and solitude beneath those big pine trees. I did not worry whether someone was looking for us. I just followed my mother into the trees. I noticed that the pine trees had a very strong, pleasing smell and that the pine cones were everywhere. I was especially impressed with the green ones still hanging on the tree.

Now when I see a pine tree with green pine cones, I am transported to a certain war vignette. I remember the stone bomb shelters in the forest where my mother and I hid. We found an army outfit and stayed with them for a while for protection. As a result, when I am in presence of a green pine cone, I recall the peace and silence that was so welcome when I found it long ago. I often wonder how I could have had these feeling at such a young age. Despite the horrors of the war, I somehow recognized peace, although I did not know its meaning then.

Even today after Sunday Mass, I take time to be with the pine cones hanging from the huge tree at the side of the church. I leave the service a few minutes early to find peace and quiet with my pine cones. This continues to be one of my better Sunday moments.

Green pine cones have more personality. When I touch them, they seem to be stronger and put together more tightly. Some years ago I kept a green one on my desk to see what would happen. I thought that it might stay green and tight, but to my surprise, the pine cone continued to evolve. Eventually, it turned brown and opened just like the ones on the ground. This made me aware that aging, whether of people or of pine cones, cannot be stopped.

Now that I am a senior citizen, it is easy to slow down and reflect on my life. This is something that is enjoyable for me. However, I do not think about what could have been, but rather how everything worked out. All in all, I cannot complain about my ride. Sometimes it was bumpy and unpredictable, but nothing that I could not take care of at the time. Now that I am retired, I can take more time to see what is around me. I am much more aware of natural beauty that was not as important earlier. I can acknowledge that when the wind caresses my face, it feels good. I can also enjoy the fragrance of different flowers.

I enjoy my retired life. It gives me time to reflect and to see life in front of me moving at a slower pace. Time is not as important any more. When I want to do something, the finish is within my control. No one is around to hurry me or to add pressure. It is a nice feeling. The main concern about being a senior citizen is health. When I was younger, health was not a very important topic for me. Now it is on my mind more, but I'm not sure why. Perhaps it's because I do not have professional ambitions now, so I have more time to think about other things.

I remember being a young lad of 14 and looking at my father coming home from his office. I thought how smart he must be because of his age and his life experience. Now that I am his age and more, I realize that he must have encountered many situations where he did not know what to do. He was often "flying by the seat of his pants," as aviators say when they take their first solo flight. I wonder if young people looking at me have similar thoughts.

When I was young, I had opinions that I still hold true. To this day, I have no fear of death. I don't know if it is because of my experiences during World War II, but death is just part of my life. Some of my friends, as well as my children, have difficulties understanding that I do not cry or mourn anyone's death. For me, it is just a natural fact that no one can escape. I felt that way about my parents' deaths. That is not to say that I don't miss them. Instead, death to me is more like having friends who have gone far away and knowing I cannot reach them at this time.

Reflecting on my childhood, I have interesting memories. At one time I thought that I was the only person made of flesh and blood and that everyone else was made of *papier-mâché*. It was an interesting thought, but not very realistic. I also had the feeling that nothing was impossible for me. However, I thought that the environment I was in was not conducive to that idea. Perhaps that is why at a very young age I decided that moving to the United States was imperative for me.

It is ironic, but with all my travels to different countries, the country in which I have stayed the longest is the United States. In the beginning when I heard the *Star Spangled Banner*, I had a hard time deciding if it were also mine or if I were still attached to the anthems of the other countries. It was a funny feeling that I did not have control over.

Freedom is very important to me. Freedom, a word that has different connotations for people, became more important to me when I came to the United States. In Europe, it was a normal and accepted fact that I had freedom. However, when I came to the United States, I became very much aware of the word because it was discussed so often. All of a sudden, freedom became more complicated than I had thought. In my eyes, people were often behaving in inappropriate ways in the name of freedom. I had difficulties understanding the idea that anything could be considered acceptable as long as it was under the name of freedom. For me, my freedom stops when it begins to infringe on someone else's. So my philosophy is that freedom needs comprehensive principles.

After I became a citizen of the United States, I realized that many words have very definite political connotations. I suppose that I never embraced the narrow definitions of those words. That is perhaps why, during my working life, whenever I was in a group, I felt that I did not have anything in common with others. Most people take this country for granted. They do not realize that it is the only country that has a Constitution which to this day is still valid and performing as it should.

I cannot understand the mind-set that is so prevalent in distinguishing various American backgrounds. When I became an American, I considered myself a citizen and nothing else. My birth country should not add any label to my citizenship. This is why I cannot comprehend the idea of anyone being called a Polish-American or an African-American, or any other type of American. It does not make any sense to me. Certainly it is not very conducive to eradicating discrimination if one is reminded each time that he is not really a full citizen of this country. I do not mean that one has to forget his origins or his traditions. One can celebrate any tradition and still be an American. Perhaps I am wrong, but many times I do not fit in, nor do I have much in common with preconceived thoughts. However, I know that I love this country.

One very important difference I noticed when I came to the United States was the family relationship. I never thought of exploring it until, of course, it was too late. I can see now that my relationship with my father was nothing compared to the relationships children here have. My father never played with me. In this country, fathers and sometimes mothers play ball with their children. But I have to be fair: I was never home for very long. I was always going somewhere else, so maybe it was difficult to have the type of family life that exists here. That said, people don't miss what they don't know.

For me, just as for my parents, World War II disturbed my taking advantage of being a child. As a result, I never got close to my dad. Some could argue that during the twelve years that we were together as a family, I had enough time to repair the distance between us. I cannot feel sorry for myself and I don't, but there are facts that I cannot just ignore.

When I think about my parents, now that they are gone, I realize that I did not take advantage of their love. I did not know how. I was too busy going to school and doing what was expected of me. Having parents was natural, and I thought, "Doesn't everyone have parents?"

I wish that my father were still alive, because I have so many questions for him. After his death, I discovered that he had been in the London Blitz during World War II. I had been told that he was in the Polish Air Force, but that was all. I was proud of him then, but I would like to have known more at the time.

During the process of growing older, my values changed. What was important and essential before has almost no value now. This process is an on-going fact. Some experience it a little more slowly and others a little faster. I know one thing for sure: after my dad died, I realized how right he had been, although I did not want to listen to him when I was growing up. Yes, I argued with him quite often, but that was normal since at the time I was sure I knew everything.

The only regret is not being with my mom when she died. I realize now how lonely she probably felt because I was not by her side. My father was there, but I think that as a mother, she was thinking about her only child. Of course, I don't know that for a fact, but I assume that every mother would feel the same.

When I was growing up, my life was good and it did prepare me to be independent and to find solutions by myself. At the time, my youth seemed perfect. I saw a lot of countries and cultures. No one in particular shaped my thoughts. My feelings and beliefs were made up of accumulated experiences. It is only later in life that a person may find out that there were other ways. To say which way is better, I cannot.

Since I came to this country my life has been good. I do not compare my life to anyone else's to derive a positive view. The best happened to me when I embraced the family that I have now. It is not perfect, but I found through the years that we were just an average family and just as dysfunctional as any other. I tried to do the best that I knew how, but I did not have the background that children here are used to. I was not prepared for looking for excuses or blaming others when life took an abrupt turn south. So with my new-found family, I was rather intransigent. I cannot say if that was the right philosophy. I know I had enough detractors, including my father when he visited us.

I tried to instill my feelings in our children. However, I do not think I was very successful. I feel that there is, for lack of better words, a misunderstanding of the feelings between most of our children and myself. When I married Carolina, she had five children. For me, the children became my children too. There was no process of deciding if they were going to be or not. But I feel very strongly that it was not the same from the children's point of view. I can understand that, because they have a blood relationship with their biological father. I used to wonder if I would be a good father or just a stranger. The answer might come in time.

I am the lucky one. My wife is my best friend. Two of the children consider me their dad, which is a big honor for me. I don't know if I can reciprocate what they expect of me, but I do what I think is right. The question for me is, "Was I not sensitive enough to see what had to be done to have a better family relationship?" Of course, now it is too late, but I still think about it. All of the children have done well, some earlier than others, but that's life.

Throughout the years, friends and strangers alike encouraged me to write this book. People often asked me how and why I came to this country. When I gave them a synopsis, they said that my life was very interesting and that I should write about my experiences. One day I decided that I would. But it took another twenty years before I actually started to write.

I am glad I did. Writing has been therapeutic in the sense of discovering my life from a different perspective. *Through My Eyes...* has made me look at my life more closely than I was used to doing. I found out that I had feelings that I had not paid attention to. I saw my parents in a different light. My experiences now seem to be more real. I discovered that I am enjoying my life.

My question, "Did I make a difference?" is blurred now. The more mature I become, the more blurred the question becomes. In a sense, the question becomes no question at all since what has been and what is now cannot be changed.

www.ingramcontent.com/pod-product-compliance
Lightning Source LLC
Chambersburg PA
CBHW032057080426
42733CB00006B/307